RECLAIMING HUMANITY IN EDUCATION

SARAH AIONO

The Teacher's Heart: Reclaiming Humanity in Education
© 2025 Dr. Sarah Aiono

All rights reserved. No part of this publication may be reproduced, stored in a retrieval system, or transmitted in any form or by any means - electronic, mechanical, photocopying, recording, or otherwise - without prior written permission of the publisher, except in the case of brief quotations embodied in reviews or critical articles.

The moral rights of the author have been asserted. First published in 2025

ISBN (paperback): 978-0-473-76019-9
ISBN (PDF): 978-0-473-76020-5

Publisher: Taunga Auaha Publishing, Napier, New Zealand
Printed in Australia
Cover design: Author
Interior design and typesetting: Cropmarks Prepress Services

A catalogue record for this book is available from the National Library of New Zealand.

For permissions, enquiries, or bulk orders, please contact:
Taunga Auaha Publishing
Napier, New Zealand
info@longwortheducation.co.nz

Publisher's Note

In order to respect the privacy of individuals, the names of students, teachers, and schools referred to in the stories throughout this book are pseudonyms. Some details have also been altered or combined to protect confidentiality while preserving the authenticity of the experiences described.

Dedication

For every teacher who has carried the unseen weight of this profession, standing in the space between what children need and what the system demands, and choosing care, connection, and hope. This book is from my heart to yours, your courage, and your steadfast belief that education is, and always will be, about more than test scores.

Table of Contents

Dedication .... *iii*

Introduction .... *vii*

CHAPTER ONE: Anchoring to the Teacher Heart 1

CHAPTER TWO: Curriculum, Compliance, and the Politics of Teaching 13

CHAPTER THREE: Navigating the Gap: Policy, Leadership, and the
                 Real Work of Schools 28

CHAPTER FOUR: Thriving as a Teacher – What We Need to Do Our
                 Best Work 37

CHAPTER FIVE: Thriving Students: Seeing Progress Differently 45

CHAPTER SIX: Reclaiming Your Agency 55

CHAPTER SEVEN: Teaching as a Human Science 65

CHAPTER EIGHT: An Invitation To Teachers 77

Introduction

This book was born out of conversations whispered in staff rooms, spoken in frustration at the end of long days, and shared in the quiet solidarity that exists among teachers who understand both the profound joy and the unrelenting weight of this profession. It is for the educators who feel their work has been narrowed to benchmarks and scripts, who wonder what happened to the creativity and humanity that drew them to teaching in the first place.

We are living in a moment of profound tension in education. Here in Aotearoa New Zealand, and indeed across the globe, teachers are navigating political cycles that swing between competing ideologies, each carrying a new reform agenda, each promising that this time they have the answer. The result is a profession too often treated as a political football rather than a cornerstone of society. Policies shift, curricula are rewritten, and evidence is wielded as a weapon rather than a tool. Meanwhile, classrooms remain filled with children whose needs cannot be standardised: children who are joyful, exhausted, hungry, anxious, curious, playful, traumatised, neurodivergent, creative, and complex, all at once.

This book is not about adding more to your plate. It is about reconnecting you to your teacher heart: the relationships, the small wins, the sparks of curiosity, the deep knowing that teaching is an act of hope. It is not a manual or a checklist. It is a conversation, a weaving together of stories, research, and reflection, to affirm that your instincts are right: education is about people, not programmes.

You will not find easy answers in these pages. Instead, you will find provocations, questions, and reminders that teaching is a profoundly human profession that thrives not through compliance, but through courage, creativity, and connection. You will find affirmation that evidence matters, but so does heart; that standards matter, but so does joy; that while systems may try to measure our impact in data points, the true measure of our work lies in the lives we touch.

This is a book for the tired but hopeful teacher, the courageous leader trying to hold space for their staff, and the educator who needs reminding that they are not alone. It is both a mirror and a lifeline: an invitation to anchor yourself to the teacher heart that brought you here, and to find again the deep well of purpose that keeps you in this work.

Even when it feels impossibly hard.

Chapter One

Anchoring to the Teacher Heart

The Girl Who Slept in the Library Corner

She was six years old, third of four siblings, three at school, one still at home. Every day, they arrived together, sometimes with bags, often without shoes, never with lunch. Her hair was thick with head lice. We suspected they got themselves to school, their parents absent or unable to manage. Her father was a Mongrel Mob member, patched up, physically imposing, and known in the community. Her mother looked lifeless, drained by a reality we couldn't see but could only guess at.

This little girl struggled with her literacy, not because she couldn't learn, but because she was exhausted. Some afternoons she would curl up in the beanbags in our library corner and fall asleep, the hum of classroom activity swirling around her.

I didn't wake her. Instead, I let her sleep. I saw her need for rest as more pressing than the literacy block I was supposed to run. I rearranged her reading sessions to fit around her naps, because I knew that learning could wait; her wellbeing couldn't.

One day, she fell asleep so deeply that when the bell rang, she didn't stir. I gently woke her, told her it was time to go home, and then rushed off to a staff meeting, assuming as I always did, that she'd head home with her siblings as usual.

At 4:20 that afternoon, her dad, patched and puffed up, stormed into school, yelling her name. His presence was intimidating; you couldn't help but feel the tension shift when he walked in. He hadn't found her at home.

I rushed back to the classroom and found her still asleep in the library corner, oblivious to it all. Her Dad strutted into my room, picked her up like a sack of potatoes, slung her over his shoulder, and walked out.

That moment has never left me. School was her sanctuary: a place of warmth, safety, and rest. Sometimes, the most educationally sound thing I could do was simply to let her sleep.

Why the Teacher Heart Matters

Teaching, at its core, is profoundly human work. It is relational, moral, and emotional. Every interaction we have with our students carries weight, not just academically, but neurologically and developmentally. The "teacher heart" - our capacity for empathy, care, attunement, and relational responsiveness - is not a soft add-on to our practice. It is the bedrock upon which effective teaching and learning are built. Without it, even the most technically proficient pedagogy risks becoming mechanical and disconnected from the lived realities of our students.

And yet, in today's policy environment, heart-led teaching is often viewed with suspicion or even derision. The language of education has shifted steadily towards managerialism: dominated by evidence hierarchies, compliance measures, and data- driven accountability systems. In this framing, only what is countable "counts." Words such as "fidelity," "structured," "benchmarks," and "evidence" dominate professional conversations, subtly positioning relational teaching and responsiveness as unscientific, inefficient, or even indulgent. When policymakers speak of "raising standards," it is almost always synonymous with standardisation, as though sameness equates to quality.

We hear refrains like: *"You can't measure belonging."* And yet, this misses a crucial truth: just because something is difficult to quantify does not mean it is insignificant. Indeed, some of the most impactful aspects of teaching - belonging, trust, safety, and connection - are those least visible in test scores but most visible in children's lives.

Neuroscience, psychology, and decades of educational research affirm what teachers instinctively know: learning is an embodied and relational act.

Bruce Perry's (2006) Neurosequential Model of Development articulates this clearly: before children can engage in reasoning or abstract thought, their nervous systems must first feel safe and regulated. His "3 Rs" - *Regulate, Relate, Reason* - offer a powerful lens for understanding why relational teaching is not a luxury but a neurological necessity. If a child's stress response is activated, the prefrontal cortex, the seat of higher-order thinking, literally goes offline. Without safety, there is no learning.

This is echoed in Stephen Porges' Polyvagal Theory (2018), which demonstrates how cues of relational warmth and safety activate the parasympathetic nervous system, calming the body and priming the brain for engagement. Similarly, Daniel Siegel's (2012) work on interpersonal neurobiology highlights that teacher-student interactions can "co-regulate" emotional states, synchronising neural patterns in ways that directly support cognitive growth. These findings reaffirm that the emotional climate we create is not ancillary to learning, it is the very soil in which it grows.

When we ignore the teacher heart, we risk reducing teaching to a transactional delivery model, moving content from teacher to student without attending to the conditions that make that transfer possible. Schools are not factories, and education cannot be meaningfully reduced to throughput metrics (OECD, 2025). Learning is deeply human. It happens in contexts of trust, belonging, and mutual respect. Teachers who bring relational depth to their practice are not "soft"; they are working in alignment with what research across neuroscience, psychology, and pedagogy tells us is both effective and ethical.

This is not indulgence. It is not sentimentality. It is rigorously supported by evidence. In fact, if we divorce education from the heart, we undermine the very conditions that allow evidence-based strategies to function. A literacy lesson is meaningless if the child is too anxious to pay attention. Formative feedback is irrelevant if the learner feels unsafe to take risks. Explicit instruction may clarify knowledge, but without relational trust, it fails to inspire curiosity or persistence. Heart is not in competition with evidence; it is the precondition for its success.

Teacher Identity and Purpose

Educational thinkers like Palmer (2017) have long argued that technique alone does not define good teaching. What matters most is the teacher's sense of identity and integrity, which shape every decision, every relationship, and every moment of practice.

However, teacher identity is not a static concept; it is dynamic, evolving through personal experience, institutional context, and sociopolitical pressures. It encompasses how teachers see themselves in relation to their students, their profession, and the moral purpose underpinning their work (Beauchamp & Thomas, 2009). This identity shapes every pedagogical choice we make, from how we respond to a distressed child to how we navigate policy mandates that conflict with our professional judgement.

Research confirms that strong professional identity correlates with higher resilience, efficacy, and job satisfaction (Day & Gu, 2014). Teachers who feel connected to their "why" are more likely to withstand external pressures and remain adaptable in the face of reform. In contrast, when identity is eroded - when teachers are asked to prioritise compliance over relational care or scripted delivery over professional autonomy - their sense of agency diminishes (Santoro, 2018; Hakanen et al., 2022).

This is not simply about individual mindset; it is also systemic. Teacher identity is nurtured in environments that value trust, autonomy, and professional dialogue (OECD, 2025). When schools create cultures of shared purpose and relational trust, teachers report greater alignment between their values and their daily work, fuelling what Fullan (2020) calls "deep moral professionalism."

Moreover, identity is inseparable from relationships. A teacher's authenticity - the alignment between personal values, beliefs about learning, and daily practice - creates a powerful modelling effect for students. Kelchtermans (2009) frames this as "vulnerability as a strength": when teachers bring their whole selves into their classrooms, they humanise education, demonstrating integrity and compassion in ways that transcend content delivery.

Yet, identity is also constantly negotiated in response to external demands. Recent studies highlight how frequent policy shifts, prescriptive curricula, and accountability regimes contribute to what Santoro (2018) calls demoralisation: the emotional toll of being unable to enact what teachers know is good and right for their students. Unlike burnout, which is often framed as individual weakness, demoralisation is a structural condition, arising when systems constrain teachers from acting in alignment with their values.

This is why anchoring to the teacher heart is not merely about emotional wellbeing. It is about sustaining professional integrity in a landscape that often challenges it. Teachers must be empowered to see themselves as moral agents, capable of filtering policy through their ethical compass and contextual expertise. Doing so is not an act of resistance alone, it is an act of fidelity to the deeper purpose of education: the flourishing of young people.

As Kelchtermans reminds us, teacher identity is shaped by community, by stories shared in staffrooms, and by the collegial trust that allows teachers to navigate complexity together. Schools that intentionally invest in these relational infrastructures, such as collaborative inquiry, peer mentoring, reflective dialogue, do more than boost morale: they affirm that teaching is a deeply human profession grounded in shared purpose.

The teacher heart, then, is not a sentimental metaphor. It is a professional necessity. A compass guiding us toward practices that are evidence-informed, ethically grounded, and attuned to the lived realities of our students. When we are anchored in our identity and purpose, we resist being reduced to technicians. We remain whole educators, able to integrate research and humanity in service of the children entrusted to us.

Protecting the Teacher Heart

Anchoring ourselves to our teacher hearts is not passive work; it requires deliberate attention, reflection, and supportive practices. What follows are evidence-based strategies that are both research grounded and practical ways to sustain our identity and purpose in teaching.

Revisit Your "Why"

Reconnecting with your purpose is a powerful buffer against the emotional fatigue of teaching. Ryan and Deci's (2020) concept of *self-concordant goals*, those aligned with our core values, demonstrates that when we operate from intrinsic motivation, our work feels more meaningful and energising. For teachers, this means regularly reflecting on the reasons we entered the profession and identifying the moments that affirm our impact. These acts of "purpose recall" not only combat the sense of futility that can arise under high-stakes accountability pressures but also reinforce identity coherence: the alignment between who we are and what we do (Day & Gu, 2014). Simple rituals, such as ending the week by journaling one interaction or breakthrough that rekindled your "why," shift attention from deficit-driven narratives to purpose-driven practice. Over time, these reflections create a protective narrative of meaning that strengthens resilience in the face of policy churn and external scrutiny.

▶ MICRO-MOMENTS OF JOY

Barbara Fredrickson's Broaden-and-Build Theory highlights how small positive emotions accumulate to build lasting psychological resources (Fredrickson, 2001, 2013). In teaching, noticing and savouring micro-moments - a child's spontaneous laughter, a "lightbulb" moment of understanding, or a thank-you note from a student - reorients our attention away from the stressors that so often dominate our cognitive load. Psychological research shows that our brains are wired with a "negativity bias," meaning negative events are more salient and sticky than positive ones (Rozin & Royzman, 2001). Intentionally capturing joyful micro-moments counters this bias, rewiring neural pathways towards optimism and broadening our emotional bandwidth. Keeping a "joy journal" or sharing a "best moment of the week" with colleagues creates a culture of noticing what is working, even in difficult contexts. This practice is not frivolous. It is a scientifically validated way of building emotional endurance and maintaining hopefulness within demanding educational landscapes (Fredrickson, 2001, 2013; Rozin & Royzman, 2001).

▶ BOUNDARIES AS CARE

Boundaries are often misunderstood in education, framed as reluctance or lack of dedication, when in reality they are a form of professional stewardship. Skaalvik and Skaalvik's (2021) longitudinal research demonstrates that teachers who lack control over workload boundaries experience higher rates of emotional exhaustion and intent to leave the profession. Protecting time and energy is an ethical act because it safeguards our capacity to show up fully for our students. Prioritisation tools, such as distinguishing between urgent and important tasks (Covey, 2020), help teachers focus on what truly matters: core teaching work and relational interactions that drive learning. Learning to say a "strategic no" to non- essential demands, such as unnecessary paperwork or meetings detached from classroom impact, preserves energy for high-value work. In schools where leadership models this behaviour, cultures shift to view boundary-setting not as resistance but as professionalism in action.

▶ SELF-COMPASSION PRACTICES

Self-compassion is more than a personal wellbeing strategy; it is a professional survival skill (Neff, 2021). Teaching is inherently relational and exposes us daily to vulnerability, uncertainty, and imperfection. Neff's model focused on self- kindness, recognition of shared humanity, and mindfulness, offers a framework for reframing failure or difficulty without harsh self-criticism. For example, after a challenging lesson, a self-compassionate response might sound like: *"This was tough, but I'm not alone in this. Many teachers experience moments like this. What can I learn and carry forward?"* Research shows that self-compassion correlates with lower cortisol levels, reduced anxiety, and greater persistence in the face of setbacks (Neff & Germer, 2018). In teaching, where emotional labour is intense and mistakes feel highly visible, these practices restore equilibrium and help us recover quickly rather than ruminate unproductively.

▶ COLLEGIAL CONNECTION

Teaching is too often described as solitary work, but it thrives within relational ecosystems. Hakanen et al. (2022) identify collegial trust and shared purpose as critical predictors of teacher wellbeing and retention. Connection is both protective and generative: it buffers against stress while also fuelling professional dialogue that refines practice. Intentional spaces for collegiality, whether informal coffee catch-ups, peer mentoring pairs, or structured story- sharing sessions, reinforce that teaching is a communal endeavour rather than an individual struggle. Collective efficacy research (Goddard et al., 2015) shows that when teachers believe their colleagues share responsibility and capability for student success, both morale and outcomes improve. Investing time in collegial relationships is not a distraction from core work; it is part of the infrastructure that sustains it, enabling us to draw strength from each other in ways that no individual self-care strategy can replicate.

Teaching With Heart

Anchoring to our teacher hearts isn't naïve. It is an act of courage and professionalism. In an era increasingly defined by metrics, compliance, and standardisation, choosing to lead with heart is a radical reaffirmation of what education is truly for: human flourishing. It is how we sustain ourselves as educators and how we create classrooms where children are seen not merely as data points or test-takers, but as complex, vibrant learners shaped by context, culture, and lived experience.

Heart-led teaching does not stand in opposition to rigour or evidence. On the contrary, it enacts the best of both. Neuroscience and psychology affirm what teachers intuitively know: learning is relational and embodied. Before the prefrontal cortex engages in reasoning or problem-solving, the nervous system must feel safe. Before children can risk error or stretch themselves cognitively, they must trust that they belong. By approaching teaching through a *regulate, relate, and reason* framework, (Perry, 2006), wellbeing is not an "extra"; it is the prerequisite for every other educational aspiration.

This perspective reframes our priorities. It means that pausing to comfort a distressed child, investing time in building connection, or even letting a tired six-year-old sleep is not a diversion from "the real teaching", it *is* real teaching. These moments lay the neurological and relational foundations upon which literacy, numeracy, and every "academic" skill depend. As culturally responsive pedagogies remind us, identity and belonging are inseparable from achievement (Bishop 2019).

Teaching with heart also demands discernment. It challenges us to critically filter policy, pedagogy, and research through the lens of humanity. It invites us to ask: *Does this practice serve my students' holistic development? Does it align with my professional integrity?* Evidence is indispensable, but without context and compassion, it risks becoming hollow. When we teach with heart, we bring evidence alive. Not as scripts to follow, but as tools to be adapted in response to the children before us.

In doing so, we reclaim teaching as both intellectual and moral work. We resist the reduction of our role to technicians delivering predetermined content and instead embrace our identity as responsive professionals - people who hold both expertise and empathy, analysis and care. This is the balance that sustains education systems capable of preparing children not just to perform, but to thrive in an uncertain and interconnected world.

Teaching with heart ultimately calls us back to our purpose: to nurture children as whole humans. It reminds us that academic progress is inseparable from safety, connection, and joy. It is in the quiet, relational acts: the encouraging smile, the patient explanation, the moment we let a child rest, that the true work of teaching resides. These moments are invisible to performance dashboards, but they shape lives in profound ways.

Anchoring to our teacher hearts is therefore both a personal and collective imperative. It sustains our sense of meaning, buffers us against burnout, and reaffirms that education is not merely about transmitting knowledge but about cultivating capacity, resilience, and hope. When we teach with heart, we choose to see beyond tests and targets to the enduring impact we have on children's sense of self and possibility.

And sometimes, that begins in the simplest acts: sitting beside a child who feels unseen, laughing with a class at an unexpected moment, or letting a tired six-year-old sleep in the corner of the library because we understand that learning will wait. Her need for rest cannot.

Chapter One References:

Beauchamp, C., & Thomas, L. (2009). Understanding teacher identity: An overview of issues in the literature and implications for teacher education. *Cambridge Journal of Education, 39*(2), 175–189. https://doi.org/10.1080/03057640902902252

Bishop, R. (2019). *Teaching to the North-East: Relationship-based learning in practice.* NZCER Press.

Covey, S. R. (2020). *The 7 habits of highly effective people* (30th anniversary ed.). Simon & Schuster.

Day, C., & Gu, Q. (2014). *Resilient teachers, resilient schools: Building and sustaining quality in testing times.* Routledge. https://doi.org/10.4324/9781315833720

Fredrickson, B. L. (2001). The role of positive emotions in positive psychology: The Broaden-and-Build theory of positive emotions. *American Psychologist, 56*(3), 218–226. https://doi.org/10.1037/0003-066X.56.3.218

Fredrickson, B. L. (2013). Positive emotions broaden and build. In P. Devine & A. Plant (Eds.), *Advances in experimental social psychology* (Vol. 47, pp. 1–53). Academic Press. https://doi.org/10.1016/B978-0-12-407236-7.00001-2

Fullan, M. (2020). *Deep learning: Engage the world change the world* (2nd ed.). Corwin.

Goddard, R. D., Goddard, Y. L., & Tschannen-Moran, M. (2015). A theoretical and empirical analysis of the roles of instructional leadership, teacher collaboration, and collective efficacy beliefs in support of student learning. *American Journal of Education, 121*(4), 501–530. https://doi.org/10.1086/681925

Hakanen, J. J., Peeters, M. C. W., & Schaufeli, W. B. (2022). Different types of employee well-being across time and their relationships with job crafting. *Journal of Occupational Health Psychology, 27*(1), 77–91. https://doi.org/10.1037/ocp0000289

Kelchtermans, G. (2009). Who I am in how I teach is the message: Self-understanding, vulnerability and reflection. *Teachers and Teaching, 15*(2), 257–272. https://doi.org/10.1080/13540600902875332

Neff, K. (2021). *Fierce self-compassion: How women can harness kindness to speak up, claim their power, and thrive*. Harper Wave.

Neff, K. D., & Germer, C. K. (2018). The Mindful Self-Compassion workbook: A proven way to accept yourself, build inner strength, and thrive. Guilford Press.

OECD. (2025). *Education for human flourishing: Reimagining the future of education and skills for the 21st century*. OECD Publishing. Retrieved from: https://www.oecd.org/content/dam/oecd/en/about/projects/edu/hpst/Human-flourishing-brochure-V5.pdf/_jcr_content/renditions/original./Human-flourishing-brochure-V5.pdf

Palmer, P. J. (2017). *The courage to teach: Exploring the inner landscape of a teacher's life* (20th anniversary ed.). Jossey-Bass.

Perry, B. D. (2006). Applying principles of neurodevelopment to clinical work with maltreated and traumatized children. In N. Boyd Webb (Ed.), *Working with traumatized youth in child welfare* (pp. 27–52). Guilford Press.

Porges, S. W. (2018). *The pocket guide to the Polyvagal Theory: The transformative power of feeling safe*. W. W. Norton.

Rozin, P., & Royzman, E. B. (2001). Negativity bias, negativity dominance, and contagion. *Personality and Social Psychology Review, 5*(4), 296–320. https://doi.org/10.1207/S15327957PSPR0504_2

Ryan, R. M., & Deci, E. L. (2020). *Self-determination theory: Basic psychological needs in motivation, development, and wellness*. Guilford Press.

Santoro, D. A. (2018). *Demoralized: Why teachers leave the profession they love and how they can stay*. Harvard Education Press.

Siegel, D. J. (2012). *The developing mind: How relationships and the brain interact to shape who we are* (2nd ed.). Guilford Press.

Skaalvik, E. M., & Skaalvik, S. (2021). Teacher burnout and teacher self-efficacy: Relations and consequences. *Teaching and Teacher Education, 105*, 103395. https://doi.org/10.1016/j.tate.2021.103395

Chapter Two
CURRICULUM, COMPLIANCE, AND THE POLITICS OF TEACHING

Silenced in the Name of Standards

As a young Resource Teacher of Learning and Behaviour (RTLB), I attended our annual national conference in New Plymouth. That year, the gathering carried a sense of anticipation: the Minister of Education, Anne Tolley, was arriving to announce a major policy shift. Before her arrival, our RTLB Association president addressed us with instructions that set the tone. There would be no questions from the floor, no visible signs of dissent, no lack of applause. We were to sit quietly, listen politely, and clap on cue.

The announcement was the introduction of National Standards, framed around the aspirational promise that every student would leave school with at least NCEA Level 2.

Tolley's message was clear: "If students have these foundation skills in literacy and numeracy, they will be able to learn across all areas of the school curriculum and will be on track to get at least NCEA Level 2" (New Zealand Government, 2009).

For the students on my caseload, this was devastating. These were learners with complex, often overwhelming needs. Through the IEP process, their teachers and

I worked relentlessly to support progress and celebrate it when it came. But their achievements could not be captured by an input-output model like National Standards. However hard they tried, these children would always be categorised as "below" or "well below."

I remember sitting in that lecture theatre with a sinking feeling in my stomach. Not only was a policy being imposed that ignored the lived realities of our most vulnerable learners, but we, the professionals closest to them, were silenced. We were not permitted to speak, question, or even quietly signal disagreement.

Yet, in that moment, our president found a way to resist. With quiet grace, she thanked the Minister for sharing her vision and then added, pointedly, that she would be happy to introduce her to the students she worked with. Students for whom Level 2 NCEA would never be possible, no matter how the targets were framed. Her words hung in the air: a subtle but powerful reminder of the children the policy had already forgotten.

The Politics of Curriculum: A Moving Target

Curriculum should be a roadmap for learning, a framework that guides teachers and inspires possibilities for students. Yet too often, it becomes narrowed to targets and templates. Instead of being anchored in a coherent, bipartisan vision that endures beyond election cycles, curriculum reform is repeatedly rewritten to score ideological points with voters.

This short-termism erodes stability for both teachers and students. Each change brings with it new documentation, new compliance demands, and a tacit message: what you did before was wrong. The energy poured into implementing yet another mandated shift is energy diverted away from teaching itself. Instead of deepening practice, we are often forced into shallow adaptation, forever reinterpreting and re-training for the "next thing."

In Aotearoa New Zealand, we have seen this pattern play out in real time. The 2023 version of Te Mātaiaho, the refresh of The New Zealand Curriculum, was designed with localised curriculum at its core. It offered flexibility and responsiveness, encouraging schools to weave in their community's stories, aspirations, and cultural identities. It recognised that effective teaching is not one-size-fits-all but rooted in place and people.

Yet almost as soon as Te Mātaiaho began to be unpacked by the profession, policy shifted again. The 2023-elected government's move back toward a singular, standardised "national curriculum" reflects a return to centralised control. It sends a clear message: uniformity is valued over context. This shift risks stripping away one of our greatest strengths: curriculum designed to be relevant to *our* children, their whānau, and their communities.

One-Size-Fits-All: The Flaw of Standardisation

A "one-size-fits-all" curriculum is not just misguided; it is pedagogically unsound. No two classrooms are the same. Within a single room, we may have children who are thriving academically alongside those facing trauma, neurodiversity, language barriers, or socio-economic hardship. To treat them as though they all operate from the same starting blocks is to wilfully ignore what decades of developmental psychology and learning science have taught us: differentiation is not optional. It is essential.

The legacy of National Standards, introduced in 2010 under the John Key-led National Government, offers a stark reminder of this. Promoted as a means to provide clear accountability and lift achievement in literacy and numeracy, National Standards set rigid benchmarks in reading, writing, and mathematics against which every child was measured. Each student was labelled *"above," "at," "below,"* or *"well below"* standard.

On the surface, this appeared simple and transparent. In reality, it created an audit culture within New Zealand schools: a system where measurement overshadowed meaning. Teachers were compelled to spend disproportionate time on assessing, moderating, and reporting rather than teaching, while schools became increasingly focused on producing data that satisfied compliance requirements rather than nurturing authentic learning (Thrupp, 2017).

There are several damaging effects of a standardised approach. These include:

- **Curriculum narrowing:** Non-core subjects such as the arts, science, and social studies are marginalised in favour of relentless drilling of "the basics." This shift particularly disadvantages students for whom broader curriculum engagement, such as through creative or inquiry-based learning, is an essential pathway into literacy and numeracy (Thrupp, 2013).

- **Labelling and self-concept:** Children internalise their results, with those labelled "below" or "well below" often developing fixed negative beliefs about their intelligence. Teachers report six-year-olds describing themselves as "dumb" based purely on their standard placement. Thrupp (2017) argued that such deficit labelling was not only demotivating but also entrenched inequities, disproportionately affecting Māori, Pasifika, and students from low socio- economic communities.

- **Teacher workload and morale:** Compliance demands escalate, with extensive time spent gathering and moderating data rather than differentiating teaching. The performative culture erodes teacher autonomy and professional trust, creating what Thrupp identified as pressures to game the system, where assessment judgements could be subtly shifted to meet expectations.

Even after National Standards were abolished in 2017, their effects linger. The students in our classrooms today, particularly those now navigating the NCEA system at secondary school, are the cohort shaped by the National Standards era. Their formative schooling years were defined by deficit-focused reporting, narrowed curriculum experiences, and a climate that prioritised measurement over meaning.

And yet, in the years since, we have not given alternative models, the very approaches favoured internationally, enough time to flourish. Countries leading global education discussions, from Finland to Singapore, focus less on rigid benchmarking and more on broad, future-focused learning: creativity, collaboration, socio-emotional skills, and adaptability (OECD, 2025). Even jurisdictions like Scotland, with its Curriculum for Excellence, have sought to balance core competencies with holistic learner development.

Te Mātaiaho, prior to the latest refreshment, promised this shift towards the future-focused approach adopted by other world-leading global education leaders. Now, New Zealand risks cycling back toward the standardisation mindset, as if the answer to past failures is simply to double down on the same strategies. Yet as Thrupp (2017) has argued, standardisation is not equipped to resolve the deep complexities of educational inequities. In fact, attempts to impose uniformity often end up reinforcing those very inequities rather than addressing them.

Carol Tomlinson's (2014) work on differentiated instruction underscores that real equity comes from *responsiveness*, not sameness. It means allowing teachers to exercise professional discretion to adapt for readiness, interest, and need. Yet the residue of National Standards continues to pull teaching toward a compliance mindset, where professional judgement is constrained by data demands and political rhetoric around "back to basics."

This leaves teachers in a constant tension: do we honour our expertise and meet children where they are, or do we default to the mandates of standardisation? It is in these moments that our "teacher hearts" are tested most deeply.

If we are serious about equity, we must break this cycle. We must resist equating fairness with uniformity and instead embrace curriculum approaches - like Te Mātaiaho's original intent - that trust teachers to blend national direction with local relevance, holistic pedagogy, and differentiated practice. The children we teach now deserve better than to remain the products of a system still haunted by the limitations of National Standards.

The Danger of Viewing Teachers as "Last-Link Implementers"

There is a quiet but insidious narrative creeping into our profession: that teachers are merely the final link in an implementation chain. In this view, curriculum is designed by "experts" far removed from classrooms, and teachers are tasked only with "delivering" it faithfully, like factory workers on an assembly line. Deviation from prescribed methods is framed not as professional judgement but as failure to comply.

This framing fundamentally misrepresents what teaching is, and what it always has been. It reduces teachers to technicians: implementers of other people's ideas, stripped of the autonomy and discretion that define true professionalism. It assumes that curriculum expertise sits exclusively in policy offices or pseudo academic institutions, while dismissing the deep, context-rich knowledge teachers hold about their students, their communities, and the lived realities of learning.

A Historical Lens: From Victorian Schools to Dewey's Progressive Vision

To understand how this view persists, we must look at the historical roots of schooling. The model of education most familiar to us today owes much to Victorian-era schooling in 19th-century Britain, a time when industrialisation demanded a compliant workforce and education systems reflected this need. Classrooms became regimented spaces: rows of desks, rote learning, rigid discipline, and standardised knowledge transmission. Teachers were positioned as authority figures tasked with enforcing order and delivering content to silent, obedient pupils.

This "factory model" of education, as it is often described, mirrored the production lines of the Industrial Revolution. Its purpose was not to cultivate creativity or critical thinking but to prepare children for predictable, hierarchical roles in an industrial society. Compliance - both of students and teachers - was a feature, not a flaw.

Contrast this with the radically different vision of John Dewey, the American philosopher and educational reformer, who argued in *Democracy and Education* (1916) that schooling should be experiential, inquiry-driven, and democratic. Dewey rejected the notion of education as mere transmission of facts. Instead, he saw learning as an active, social process rooted in real-world engagement, that is, life itself, rather than the preparation for life yet to come Dewey's model positioned teachers not as enforcers of predetermined scripts but as facilitators of curiosity. Guides who connect knowledge to children's lived experience and foster their agency as learners and citizens. His ideas laid the groundwork for progressive education: schooling designed to grow adaptable, critical, and collaborative thinkers capable of thriving in complex societies.

Yet despite over a century of research supporting Dewey's principles, modern education policy often drifts back toward Victorian tendencies: control, standardisation, and "teacher-proof" curricula that prioritise compliance over responsiveness.

John Holt and the Critique of Schooling-as-Control

In the mid-20th century, educators like John Holt further challenged the assumption that learning can be manufactured through rigid instruction. In *How Children Fail* (1964), Holt argued that traditional schooling often produces fear-driven compliance rather than authentic learning. He observed that when children are coerced into fixed, scripted patterns of learning, they become adept at looking like they're learning while disengaging internally.

Holt's insights remain strikingly relevant. A system that treats teachers as last-link implementers replicates this same dynamic. Teachers, constrained by mandates and scripts, prioritise compliance because deviation is risky. They learn to teach to the test, manage outputs, and appease oversight structures rather than responding creatively to student needs. Just as Holt described students "failing" not because of lack of ability but because of the structure imposed upon them, teachers in such systems risk a loss of integrity not through lack of skill, but through policies that strip their agency.

Teaching as Complex, Relational Work

Modern learning science reinforces what Dewey and Holt intuited: teaching is not a linear "input-output" process. It is inherently relational and responsive. Education is an encounter with the unpredictable: we teach unique, singular beings who bring their own contexts, histories, and possibilities into every lesson (Biesta, 2015).

The notion of teachers as mere deliverers of content is incompatible with this reality. Children are not standardised variables. They arrive with diverse cultural identities, neurodiversities, traumas, and talents that defy rigid curricular pacing guides. No scripted lesson, no matter how well intentioned, can anticipate or adapt to the moment a child discloses fear, sparks curiosity, or challenges the premise of a task. This is where teacher expertise resides: in reading those moments and knowing when to lean in, pivot, or pause.

By treating teachers as last-link implementers, systems erase the artistry of teaching and the in-the-moment decision-making known as adaptive expertise (Hatano & Inagaki, 1986). Adaptive expertise is not about rigidly applying what works in theory, but flexibly drawing on professional knowledge to navigate the messy realities of classrooms. It is precisely this expertise that high-performing systems like Finland nurture through autonomy and trust with their teachers, rather than scripts and surveillance.

The Cost of Implementation-Driven Teaching

Framing teachers as implementers has profound consequences. It:

- **De-skills the profession:** Teachers are trained to enact predetermined programmes rather than to think critically about pedagogy. This hollows out teacher education and reduces job satisfaction.

- **Narrows learning:** Scripted fidelity discourages exploration of local histories, cultural narratives, and emergent inquiry, vital elements of responsive teaching.

- **Erodes innovation:** When teachers are evaluated on compliance rather than creativity, risk-taking disappears. New approaches are stifled before they can develop.

- **Disconnects from purpose:** Teaching becomes unsustainable when teachers are unable to act in ways that align with their professional values. Unlike exhaustion, which is often linked to workload and stress, this disconnection occurs when systemic controls override teachers' moral agency. Implementation-driven models, where fidelity to scripts is valued over professional judgement, erode the sense of meaning that sustains educators in their work.

From Holt to Robinson and Claxton: The Enduring Challenge of Control in Schooling

Holt's concerns about compliance find echoes in the work of Sir Ken Robinson and Guy Claxton. Robinson (2006) famously argued that "schools kill creativity" when they operate as industrial-era systems designed for conformity, rather than for cultivating innovation and adaptability. He warned that such models are ill-suited for a 21st- century world that demands creativity, agility, and problem-solving.

Claxton (2018), in his *Learning Power Approach*, builds on this by emphasising the importance of developing learning dispositions such as resilience, curiosity, and collaboration. He critiques the "delivery mindset" in teaching where knowledge is treated as a one-way transfer from teacher to passive student and contrasts it with an "expansive mindset," in which teachers stretch students' capacity to think, explore, and work through uncertainty.

Together, Holt, Robinson, and Claxton converge on a central truth: when systems reduce teachers to last-link implementers, they entrench fear, conformity, and surface- level learning. Conversely, when teachers are trusted as adaptive professionals, they can create learning environments that embrace uncertainty, foster curiosity, and nurture the intellectual vibrancy needed for our times.

Fear vs. Curiosity: The Psychology of Engagement

The modern learning sciences affirm these critiques. Neuroscience demonstrates that curiosity and intrinsic motivation activate the brain's reward circuitry, enhancing memory and deep learning (Kang et al., 2009). Yet environments built around compliance, surveillance, and narrow accountability suppress these same mechanisms. Under pressure to "get it right," students learn to play defensively, avoiding risk rather than embracing exploration.

When we frame teaching as implementation rather than adaptation, we inadvertently reproduce this defensive posture in teachers as well. Claxton's research (2018) suggests that when teachers are constrained by scripts and fidelity models, their practice becomes dominated by caution. The result is a narrowing of pedagogy: teachers become less experimental and less responsive to the moment, and classrooms risk becoming places where students are conditioned to wait for instructions rather than to explore, question, and wonder.

This is precisely what Ken Robinson's TED talk on creativity railed against: an education system overly focused on "right answers" and afraid of mistakes. Robinson argued that this fear of error doesn't just limit students, it also limits teachers, who operate within tightly prescribed systems that reward risk-avoidance rather than innovation (2006; 2017).

The Teacher's Role in Reclaiming Agency

Guy Claxton offers a practical antidote to this: shifting teachers from "knowledge deliverers" to learning designers who build classrooms rich in challenge, questioning, and autonomy (2018). He argues that developing students' "learning muscles" requires teachers to model those same qualities: curiosity, flexibility, and a willingness to deviate from a script in service of deeper understanding.

This aligns directly with Holt's original insight: authentic learning thrives in environments where both students and teachers are free to experiment, fail safely, and iterate. By contrast, implementation-driven models send a clear message: *stick to the plan*. Teachers constrained by such systems often experience the anguish of being unable to teach in ways they know to be best for their students.

The Risk of Flattening the Profession

Framing teachers as mere implementers ignores this historical and research-backed understanding of teaching as an intellectual, creative act. It collapses education into a linear pipeline: policy-makers decide, experts design, teachers deliver, students absorb. But education has never worked this way. Holt, Robinson, and Claxton all remind us that learning is alive, unpredictable, and human, and so is teaching.

Glimpsing the Future: The System

If we could peer into a crystal ball and glimpse the future of education under a "flattened" profession, where teachers are mere delivery agents, implementing scripts with fidelity rather than exercising judgement, what would we see?

We might see classrooms that look orderly on the surface: rows of compliant students, lessons proceeding with clinical precision, achievement data neatly plotted on dashboards. Every child follows the same pace, the same script, the same sequence. Teachers are efficient deliverers of centrally designed lessons, rewarded for their ability to follow instructions exactly as written.

But look closer. The laughter and curiosity that once animated these spaces are muted. Risk-taking has disappeared, replaced by quiet anxiety about "getting it right." Questions that deviate from the script are discouraged. Not because teachers don't care, but because they no longer have the time or autonomy to entertain them. The 'teachable moments' that once sparked wonder are passed over, sacrificed to pacing guides and fidelity checklists.

Glimpsing the Future: Students

And what of the students who pass through this system? They become adept at compliance, good at replicating what is modelled for them, but less confident in navigating ambiguity or generating new ideas. Their learning is transactional: "Do the task, get the mark, move on."

In such a system, differentiation is an afterthought, an intervention bolted on for those who "fall behind," rather than a natural feature of responsive teaching. High-needs students become casualties of standardised pacing. Gifted students, meanwhile, are stifled by lack of extension or creative challenge. Both groups, and many in between, learn to see education as something done *to* them rather than with them.

The result? Graduates who can recall content but lack the dispositions such as resilience, curiosity, critical thinking. These are not the learners the 21st century demands. They are compliant products of a system optimised for predictability and conformity, not for possibility.

Glimpsing the Future: Teachers

Teachers, too, look different in this vision. Their professional preparation has been streamlined to focus less on pedagogy, child development, or critical inquiry, and more on programme adherence. Pre-service training teaches them how to administer content efficiently, not how to interpret learning needs or design rich, contextual experiences. Teacher expertise, once rooted in deep knowledge of learners, communities, and curriculum, has been hollowed out, replaced by procedural compliance.

For teachers, the crystal ball shows a profession drained of its vitality. Workload shifts further toward surveillance and reporting: lesson fidelity checks, data audits, performance reviews based on narrow indicators. Collaboration is less about inquiry and more about alignment, ensuring every teacher is "on the same page," quite literally, in the same week of the scripted programme.

Demoralisation deepens. When teachers are prevented from doing the moral work they came into teaching to do - connecting, adapting, making nuanced decisions - they leave. Attrition accelerates. The profession becomes transactional: a short-term job rather than a sustained vocation.

What Is Lost?

In flattening teaching, we lose the relational artistry of the profession. We lose teachers' capacity to read the room, pivot in the moment, and integrate local culture, language, and identity into their practice. We lose the richness of context: the ability to take a national curriculum and weave it into something alive for a particular community.

We also lose resilience as a system. Scripted teaching may produce surface-level uniformity, but it cannot respond to crises or change. When new challenges arise such as technological disruption, societal upheaval and yes, unexpected pandemics, teachers accustomed to compliance will be ill-prepared to adapt. Flattening may create stability in the short term, but it hollows out the very adaptability that future-facing education requires.

Is This What We Want?

If this crystal ball fills you with unease, it should. Education is not a conveyor belt; it is a living ecosystem. It thrives on the diversity of teachers' expertise, on classrooms that flex and evolve, on schools that are woven into their communities. Flattening the profession risks turning a dynamic, human endeavour into a mechanised system that prepares neither children nor teachers for the complex world ahead.

The alternative is harder but far more hopeful: a profession that embraces complexity, trusts teachers as designers of learning, and equips them to balance evidence with responsiveness. This is what high-performing education systems already do: Finland, Singapore, and others build adaptive capacity not through scripts, but through teacher autonomy, professional learning communities, and a culture of trust.

The crystal ball offers us a choice. Do we accept a future of scripted uniformity, efficient but lifeless? Or do we reclaim teaching as intellectually demanding, relationally rich work. A profession that requires not only technique but also heart, judgement, and creativity?

CHAPTER TWO REFERENCES

Biesta, G. (2015). *Good education in an age of measurement: Ethics, politics, democracy.* Routledge.

Claxton, G. (2018). *The learning power approach: Teaching learners to teach themselves.* Crown House Publishing.

Dewey, J. (1916). *Democracy and education: An introduction to the philosophy of education.* Macmillan.

Hatano, G., & Inagaki, K. (1986). Two courses of expertise. In H. Stevenson, H. Azuma, & K. Hakuta (Eds.), *Child development and education in Japan* (pp. 262–272). W.H. Freeman.

Holt, J. (1964). *How children fail.* Pitman.

Kang, M. J., Hsu, M., Krajbich, I. M., Loewenstein, G., McClure, S. M., Wang, J. T.-Y., & Camerer, C. F. (2009). The wick in the candle of learning: Epistemic curiosity activates reward circuitry and enhances memory. *Psychological Science, 20*(8), 963–973. https://doi.org/10.1111/j.1467-9280.2009.02402.x

New Zealand Government. (2009, 23 October). *National Standards to benefit children and parents* [Press release]. Beehive.govt.nz. https://www.beehive.govt.nz/release/national-standards-benefit-children-and-parents

OECD. (2025). *Education for human flourishing: Reimagining the future of education and skills for the 21st century.* OECD Publishing. Retrieved from: https://www.oecd.org/content/dam/oecd/en/about/projects/edu/hpst/Human-flourishing-brochure-V5.pdf/_jcr_content/renditions/original./Human-flourishing-brochure-V5.pdf

Robinson, K. (2006). *Do schools kill creativity?* [TED Talk]. TED Conferences. https://www.ted.com/talks/ken_robinson_do_schools_kill_creativity

Thrupp, M. (2013). *Neoliberalism and school reform in New Zealand: Is there an alternative?* Waikato Journal of Education, 18(2), 7–20.

Thrupp, M. (2017). *The search for better educational standards: A cautionary tale.* Springer.

Tomlinson, C. A. (2014). *The differentiated classroom: Responding to the needs of all learners* (2nd ed.). ASCD.

Chapter Three

NAVIGATING THE GAP: POLICY, LEADERSHIP, AND THE REAL WORK OF SCHOOLS

A Volcano in South Auckland

As a young teacher with a class of thirty-two Year Twos in South Auckland, I faced daily challenges in meeting the diverse needs of my learners. Many were working at pre-level one in both academic achievement and socio-emotional development. Their needs were immediate and visible, and I could see them in every interaction, every playground disagreement, and every hesitant step towards literacy and numeracy.

Yet the work I was being asked to do by my deputy principal often did not align with those needs. I did my best to comply with management requests while quietly protecting my students from unrealistic and inappropriate learning experiences that would serve only to reinforce fragile learner identities.

One such example was a mandated unit of study on the local mountain and the life of Māori in the area prior to European arrival. I supported the kaupapa of the unit wholeheartedly. Understanding how people lived before colonisation is essential to appreciating the history and cultural richness of the land. But the content, as prescribed, was far removed from what my students could meaningfully access.

What they were interested in was the fact that they lived near a volcano. A real one. This sparked their curiosity in ways that a set of worksheets on pre-colonial settlement simply could not. So, I navigated the policy and the practical realities. I met the official unit expectations on paper, producing the required artefacts for my deputy principal.

But in our actual classroom life, we built a volcano together. We shaped it with papier- mâché, painted it, and in the final week, we made it erupt just outside the deputy principal's office. The squeals of delight that followed were my reward, and the conversations about volcanoes lasted far longer than any formal assessment would have captured.

It was a moment where my professional judgement guided me to adapt a policy-driven requirement into something that met the developmental needs of my students. It was also a reminder that effective teaching often requires this kind of navigation.

The Tension Between Policy and Practice

Stories like the volcano lesson are not mine alone. Every teacher has their own version, a time they balanced the letter of policy against the spirit of good teaching. These moments are not simply about making do; they are acts of professional judgement, often carried out quietly, with the learner's best interests at heart.

Policy, by its very nature, is generalised. It is designed to apply across a whole system, to provide consistency, set expectations, and ensure coverage. But classrooms are anything but general. They are living ecosystems, shaped by the unique mix of children who inhabit them, the communities they are part of, and the broader social, cultural, and economic realities they reflect.

When policies demand strict fidelity, teachers are faced with a dilemma. They can comply exactly as written, or they can adapt in ways that better serve their learners, but risk being seen as non-compliant. This is not a technical choice.

It is a moral one. Such dilemmas are common in educational leadership. Teachers often describe feeling caught in the middle, particularly when policy requirements do not account for the complexities of their students' needs (Leithwood et al., 2020).

Leadership as the Bridge

This is where school leadership becomes pivotal. Leaders occupy a unique position between the demands of policymakers and the lived realities of teachers and students. How they navigate that space shapes whether a policy becomes a meaningful tool or a blunt instrument. Leithwood and colleagues (2020) describe this as the leader's role in *sense-making*: the process of interpreting policy so it aligns with the school's context and purpose.

When leaders engage in thoughtful sense-making, they act as a filter. They protect staff from unnecessary noise, adapt expectations where possible, and create space for professional discretion. In these environments, policy is not experienced as a top-down mandate but as a framework within which teachers can still act with autonomy.

Conversely, when leaders transmit policy without adaptation, the work of teaching can become dominated by procedural compliance, eroding both morale and creativity (Fullan, 2019).

Effective leaders also model how to balance competing demands. They are transparent about the constraints they work under, but they do not use those constraints as an excuse to avoid adaptation. Instead, they focus on how to meet core objectives in ways that honour the professional knowledge of their teachers. This relational approach fosters trust, which is essential for collective commitment to any change initiative (Bryk & Schneider, 2002).

The Emotional Load of Policy Work

Policy is never neutral in its effect on teachers. It is carried not just in meeting minutes and planning documents, but in the emotions, energy, and professional identity of the people enacting it. For most teachers, the work is deeply tied to their sense of purpose, the moral drive to make a difference in the lives of children. Leadership decisions that enable teachers to act in ways consistent with that purpose build confidence, trust, and resilience. In contrast, when policy implementation forces teachers to act in ways that clash with their professional judgement, frustration and moral strain begin to rise. This is more than simple tiredness: it can lead to what many scholars call *moral injury* - the experience of being unable to act in accordance with one's values. Fatigue from workload or stress can often be remedied through rest, resources, or lighter schedules.

Moral injury, by contrast, strikes at the core of professional identity. It occurs when teachers are asked to act in ways that compromise the very reasons they came into teaching, creating an erosion of agency and a loss of professional integrity.

In the leadership context, recognising this distinction is critical. While exhaustion might be alleviated by practical supports, the deeper challenge is restoring trust and affirming that teachers' professional voices matter. When decision-making is stripped away and teachers are positioned as mere conduits for centrally designed programmes, the risk of moral injury intensifies.

The consequences ripple through classrooms. Teachers who feel their integrity is compromised often disengage emotionally from their work, becoming cautious rather than creative, reluctant to take risks, and more dependent on rote or compliance-driven approaches. This is not due to apathy, but because the systems around them no longer permit them to enact what they know to be right for their students. Over time, such cultures become stagnant, defined more by obedience than by dialogue, and increasingly unable to adapt to learners' diverse needs.

Leaders are pivotal in preventing this erosion of purpose. Even within mandated constraints, they can act as filters and advocates, affirming teacher expertise, inviting professional voice into policy enactment, and working collaboratively to adapt expectations to the realities of the classroom. This kind of leadership does not deny policy, but interprets it through a lens of humanity, purpose, and moral agency. In doing so, leaders send a vital message: policy may shape the framework, but it is professional trust and integrity that breathe life into education.

Policy as Living Practice

One way to reframe the policy–practice divide is to see policy as a *living practice* rather than a static set of rules. This approach draws from the idea of "policy enactment" (Ball, Maguire, & Braun, 2012), which emphasises that policy only becomes real through the interpretations and actions of those who work with it on the ground.

In this view, a policy is not fully defined until it meets the classroom. Its success depends on the teacher's ability to adapt it to the needs of their students, and on the leader's ability to create the conditions for that adaptation. A strong leader recognises that policies designed without classroom voices are, by default, incomplete. They must be shaped in context to serve learners effectively.

Seeing policy as living practice also invites teachers to see themselves as active participants in shaping its meaning. This challenges the "last-link implementer" narrative. It positions teachers as professionals engaged in dialogue with the policy, rather than as passive receivers of someone else's decisions.

Wayfinding Leadership: Navigating the Space Between Policy and Practice

For leaders in Aotearoa, the *Wayfinding Leadership* model (Spiller, Barclay-Kerr & Panoho, 2015) offers a powerful framework for navigating the complexities of education policy while staying anchored to core values. Drawing from the rich traditions of Polynesian voyaging, wayfinding leadership is not about following a rigidly plotted course, but about reading the signs, the winds, currents, stars, and swells, and adjusting the path in response to what is happening in the moment.

In the school context, "winds" might represent political shifts, "currents" could be the lived realities of teachers and learners, and "swells" might be emerging societal challenges like inequity or socio-emotional pressures. The wayfinding leader is alert to all of these forces. Rather than simply passing policy instructions downstream, they actively interpret them through the lens of local context, ensuring that the journey is both purposeful and responsive.

A Relational Compass

Wayfinding leadership positions relationships at the centre of navigation. Leaders do not stand apart as distant captains, but work within the crew, listening and adjusting in real time. In practice, this means:

- Actively engaging with teacher voice before deciding how policy will be enacted in the school.

- Being transparent about the non-negotiables and the areas where there is space for adaptation.

- Valuing the deep professional knowledge that teachers hold about their students and communities.

This relational compass keeps trust intact, even when the seas are rough. Teachers know that their leaders are not simply implementing for the sake of compliance but are working to protect the integrity of the voyage.

Holding the Vision While Adjusting the Course

A key skill in wayfinding is the ability to maintain focus on the *destination* while making constant micro-adjustments to the route. In education, this means holding fast to the ultimate purpose - the wellbeing and growth of learners - while accepting that the journey there will rarely match the straight lines drawn in policy documents.

In a mandated curriculum change, for example, a wayfinding leader may acknowledge the broad intentions of the policy while also re-sequencing content, adapting examples, or pacing implementation to ensure that it lands meaningfully for their community. These adjustments are not acts of defiance but acts of stewardship, ensuring the waka stays seaworthy and the crew stays engaged.

Embracing the Unknown

Wayfinding requires comfort with uncertainty. Leaders cannot rely solely on set maps because conditions change, and not everything is visible at the outset. The willingness to "read the ocean" mirrors the capacity to respond to emergent needs in schools, whether that is shifting support for a struggling teacher, rethinking a timetable to allow for student wellbeing initiatives, or finding creative ways to meet policy requirements without undermining local priorities.

This stands in sharp contrast to compliance-driven leadership, which often treats deviation from the plan as a problem to be corrected rather than a natural and necessary part of the voyage.

Why This Matters Now

Aotearoa's current education climate is one of rapid policy change, increased centralisation, and heightened scrutiny. For many school leaders, it can feel as though the policy "map" is being redrawn mid-voyage, often without consultation. In such a climate, the principles of wayfinding leadership - relational trust, contextual navigation, and moral purpose - are not optional extras. They are survival skills.

When leaders approach policy as navigators rather than gatekeepers, they model for their staff that professional agency still matters, that context still matters, and that the destination remains the same: thriving learners who are prepared for the complexities of life beyond school. This is not about ignoring policy, but about enacting it with integrity, humanity, and a keen eye on the horizon.

The Courage to Adapt

Ultimately, navigating the policy–practice divide requires courage on the part of both teachers and leaders. For teachers, this might mean making small but significant shifts in how a lesson is delivered to ensure that every child can access it meaningfully. For leaders, it might mean pushing back on unrealistic expectations from above or reinterpreting them in ways that protect the integrity of learning.

This courage is not about rebellion for its own sake. It is about holding fast to the purpose of education: to help young people grow into capable, curious, and compassionate human beings. When policy supports that goal, we work with it gladly. When it does not, we work around it. Not out of defiance, but out of fidelity to the deeper responsibility we hold to our students.

If the education system is to thrive, we need leaders who see their role not just as managing compliance, but as guardians of purpose. We need policies that trust the expertise of teachers, and teachers who feel safe to use that expertise. And we need to keep asking the hard question: Does this policy serve the learner in front of me, or does it serve the system? The answer to that question should guide our every decision.

CHAPTER THREE REFERENCES

Ball, S. J., Maguire, M., & Braun, A. (2012). *How schools do policy: Policy enactments in secondary schools*. Routledge.

Biesta, G. (2015). *Good education in an age of measurement: Ethics, politics, democracy*. Routledge.

Bryk, A. S., & Schneider, B. (2002). *Trust in schools: A core resource for improvement*. Russell Sage Foundation.

Fullan, M. (2019). *Nuance: Why some leaders succeed and others fail*. Corwin.

Leithwood, K., Harris, A., & Hopkins, D. (2020). Seven strong claims about successful school leadership revisited. *School Leadership & Management, 40*(1), 5–22. https://doi.org/10.1080/13632434.2019.1596077

Spiller, C., Barclay-Kerr, H., & Panoho, J. (2015). *Wayfinding leadership: Groundbreaking wisdom for developing leaders*. Huia Publishers.

Chapter Four

Thriving as a Teacher: What We Need to Do Our Best Work

Trust in Action

In my early years of teaching, I was given a class of students who had been excluded from other schools because of behavioural challenges. The room was filled with sharp eyes and quick tempers, with children who had learned that school was not a place for them. All carried invisible burdens: fractured home lives, unmet learning needs, and deep mistrust of adults. Every day was like walking on egg shells.

The most important thing I learned in those first weeks was that behaviour was not the problem I needed to solve first. Trust was. The systems around me were focused on discipline plans and academic goals, but I could see that these would crumble without a foundation of safety and connection. I knew my students would only take risks in their learning if they believed I was on their side.

That meant making small, deliberate choices that sometimes diverged from the official plan. We shifted the focus away from reading, writing and maths outcomes and while still taught, these skills were not our main priority. Instead, we gave attention to our children's sense of safety. Their ability to trust adults at school. Provided predictability through a lens of care and kindness. I took time to listen when a child was upset, even if it meant planned activities started late, or not at all. I built routines that gave them control over small parts of their day. I celebrated tiny wins that would not appear in any assessment data. Over time, we became a community. Learning began to happen not because I enforced it, but because the students felt able to engage.

This was only possible because my school leadership gave me space to respond to the realities in front of me. They trusted me to make professional decisions, and that trust was my permission to teach with heart and integrity.

The Foundations of Teacher Thriving

When we talk about what teachers need in order to thrive, the conversation often drifts toward resourcing and workload. These are critical factors, but they are not the whole picture. Thriving is not only about having more time or better tools. It is about being able to use professional knowledge in ways that align with deeply held values, while feeling supported and respected by those around us.

Research on teacher wellbeing (Day & Gu, 2010) shows that resilience is not an individual trait we either have or do not have. It is socially constructed, built through relationships, trust, and shared purpose. Thriving teachers are rarely those who operate in isolation; instead, they are part of a professional community where they can take risks, share challenges, and learn from one another without fear of judgement. In schools where leaders create a climate of psychological safety, teachers are more likely to experiment, reflect honestly on challenges, and adapt their practice for the benefit of their students.

Thriving also depends on professional permission - the trust that teachers can exercise their judgement in the moment. Permission is the opposite of a compliance culture where every decision must be checked against a script or policy before it can be acted upon. It is not about ignoring guidelines; rather, it is about interpreting them with professional insight, taking into account the unique context of the students in front of them.

Importantly, teachers are not just professionals, they are also human beings with lives outside the classroom. Most juggle family responsibilities, care for children or elderly relatives, contribute to their communities, and nurture personal interests and hobbies.

Far from being distractions, these aspects of life enrich a teacher's perspective and deepen their capacity to connect with students. A teacher who is enabled to thrive in all areas of life can bring more empathy, creativity, and stability to the classroom. When leaders recognise and support the whole person - not just the role - they foster a teaching culture that is sustainable, energising, and profoundly human.

Thriving, then, is about a holistic ecology: meaningful professional autonomy, trust- based relationships, and the recognition that teachers' wellbeing outside school fuels their effectiveness inside it. Without this balance, even the most skilled teacher will struggle to sustain the energy and commitment that great teaching demands.

Autonomy as a Core Professional Need

Before teachers can truly bring their full selves to the work, they must be trusted to use their expertise in ways that respond to the realities of their classrooms. This is where autonomy becomes central. It is the foundation that allows teachers to balance curriculum expectations with the lived experiences, cultures, and needs of their students. Without it, teaching risks becoming a mechanical delivery of prescribed content rather than a dynamic, adaptive, and deeply human profession. Autonomy empowers teachers to navigate the unpredictable nature of learning, to innovate when necessary, and to draw on their professional judgement in ways that enrich both their practice and their students' outcomes.

The Role of Autonomy in Professional Thriving

Autonomy is more than simply being left alone to "get on with it." It is the ability to make informed decisions about teaching and learning based on a deep understanding of students, the curriculum, and the broader goals of education. When teachers have autonomy, they can adapt learning experiences to match the needs of a particular class, try innovative approaches, and respond in real time to what is happening in the learning environment.

Research has consistently shown that autonomy is a key factor in job satisfaction for teachers (OECD, 2020). It provides a sense of ownership over the work and reinforces professional identity. Teachers who feel they have control over the "how" of their teaching are more motivated and engaged, which translates into richer learning experiences for students.

However, autonomy does not mean a lack of accountability. In fact, the most effective forms of autonomy are paired with collective responsibility. Teachers are empowered to make decisions within a shared vision for learning, ensuring that individual choices still align with the school's overarching goals and values. This balance is what allows innovation to flourish without creating inconsistency or confusion for students.

A culture of autonomy relies heavily on trust. Leaders must trust teachers to act in the best interests of students, and teachers must trust that leaders will support them when they take risks or encounter setbacks. Without this mutual trust, autonomy becomes fragile and easily undermined by top-down mandates or overly prescriptive policies (Le Fevre, Timperley, & Ell, 2015).

True autonomy also acknowledges that teachers bring their whole selves into their work. Professional judgement is enriched by life experience, cultural background, personal interests, and relationships outside of school. When a teacher can integrate these aspects into their practice, they are more likely to create authentic connections with students and to teach in ways that feel meaningful and sustainable.

The Whole Person Behind the Teacher

Thriving as a teacher is not only about meeting classroom demands. It's also about being recognised as a whole person. Teachers bring with them family responsibilities, community commitments, creative passions, and personal experiences that enrich their practice. These are not distractions; they add depth, empathy, and authenticity to the way we connect with students.

Yet when compliance and workload pressures dominate, teachers often slip into survival mode. Personal commitments are pushed aside, and the very qualities that make teaching relational and meaningful are eroded. A thriving teacher is one who has the space and trust to integrate their full self into their work, knowing that their humanity is a strength, not a weakness.

Leadership is crucial in making this possible. When leaders acknowledge teachers as whole people, they create a culture where life experience, cultural background, and personal strengths are seen as assets in the classroom. This support is not an "extra". it is central to sustaining energy, authenticity, and joy in teaching.

The Role of Leadership in Protecting Autonomy

Leadership is the bridge between policy expectations and classroom realities. Leaders who protect and nurture teacher autonomy are not disregarding accountability; they are reframing it (Hargreaves & Fullan, 2012). Rather than simply ensuring policies are followed to the letter, they focus on how those policies can be interpreted in ways that genuinely serve students.

This requires leaders to draw on principles of **adaptive leadership** (Heifetz, Grashow, & Linsky, 2009). Adaptive leadership recognises that schools operate in constantly changing environments where predetermined solutions are rarely sufficient. Instead of following a fixed map, leaders must balance stability with flexibility, holding fast to values and vision while adjusting course in response to emerging realities.

At its core, adaptive leadership is about mobilising people to face challenges that have no straightforward answers. It places emphasis on relational trust, dialogue, and a collective sense of purpose, ensuring that decisions are not only technically sound but also ethically grounded.

In practice, this might mean:

- Negotiating with the Ministry to adjust the timing or format of a mandated initiative so that it works meaningfully in the school's context.
- Supporting teachers to pilot new approaches in small, low-risk ways before embedding them across the school.
- Creating reflective spaces where staff can examine whether current practices align with professional ethics and the real needs of students.

When leaders enact this kind of adaptive navigation, they signal to staff that the work is not simply about compliance. It is about discerning the best path forward for their particular community, even amidst shifting demands. In doing so, they foster a culture of integrity, resilience, and collective responsibility - conditions where both teachers and learners are able to thrive.

Wellbeing as Collective Responsibility

Teacher wellbeing cannot be left to individual self-care strategies. It is shaped by the culture and structures of the school (Day & Gu, 2010; OECD, 2020). Workload expectations, meeting schedules, assessment demands, and leadership style all play a role in determining whether a teacher's day is sustainable or depleting.

Day and Gu (2010) argue that professional wellbeing is sustained when teachers feel effective and valued. This means leaders need to actively affirm teacher expertise, especially when policy pressures are high. Recognition does not always have to come in grand gestures. Simple acts like visiting classrooms to celebrate good practice, inviting teachers to share their innovations, or defending teacher decisions in external meetings can make a significant difference.

In thriving schools, wellbeing is not seen as a soft extra. It is treated as foundational to student success (Hargreaves & Fullan, 2012). The reasoning is simple: teachers who feel supported and empowered are better able to create the conditions in which students can succeed.

Thriving Teachers, Thriving Students

The relationship between teacher thriving and student thriving is reciprocal (Robinson et al., 2009). Thriving is not a luxury in education; it is a necessity. It is how we sustain ourselves in a profession that is both demanding and deeply rewarding. It is how we ensure that every child has access to the kind of teaching that sees them as more than data points or test scores.

In the end, thriving comes back to trust. Trust between teacher and student, between teacher and leader, and between schools and the communities they serve (Edmondson, 2019). When that trust is strong, policy and practice can work together rather than against each other. And when teachers thrive, everyone in the school benefits.

CHAPTER FOUR REFERENCES

Day, C., & Gu, Q. (2010). *The new lives of teachers.* Routledge. https://doi.org/10.4324/9780203840990

Edmondson, A. C. (2019). *The fearless organization: Creating psychological safety in the workplace for learning, innovation, and growth.* Wiley.

Hargreaves, A., & Fullan, M. (2012). *Professional capital: Transforming teaching in every school.* Teachers College Press.

Heifetz, R. A., Grashow, A., & Linsky, M. (2009). *The practice of adaptive leadership: Tools and tactics for changing your organization and the world.* Harvard Business Press.

Le Fevre, D. M., Timperley, H., & Ell, F. (2015). Curriculum and pedagogy: The future of teacher professional learning and development. *The Curriculum Journal, 26*(2), 1–18. https://doi.org/10.1080/09585176.2015.1045539

OECD. (2020). Teaching in Focus #34: Professional collaboration as a key support for teachers working in challenging environments. OECD Publishing. Retrieved from: https://www.oecd.org/content/dam/oecd/en/publications/reports/2020/09/professional-collaboration-as-a-key-support-for-teachers-working-in-challenging-environments_310402b3/c699389b-en.pdf

Robinson, V. M. J., Hohepa, M., & Lloyd, C. (2009). *School leadership and student outcomes: Identifying what works and why (Best Evidence Synthesis iteration)*. The University of Auckland and New Zealand Ministry of Education. Retrieved from https://www.researchgate.net/.../School-Leadership-and-Student-Outcomes-Identifying-What-Works-and-Why-Best-Evidence-Synthesis-Iteration-BES.pdf

Chapter Five

Thriving Students: Seeing Progress Differently

Measuring a Different Kind of Progress

I still remember the faces of the students in that class. They were the ones who had been excluded from other schools, sometimes more than once. Their names came with files as thick as novels, each page detailing incidents, behaviour plans, and official reports. By the time they arrived in my classroom, they had heard, explicitly and implicitly, that they were "behind", "a problem", or "too difficult".

If I had relied only on standardised assessments, every report I sent home would have reinforced those messages. The data would have told the same story over and over again - that these children were failing. But in the day-to-day reality of our classroom, I could see something different. A boy who once refused to write his name was now filling a page with sentences. A girl who had barely spoken in her first term was presenting her ideas to the class. There were fewer physical fights, meltdowns and arguments. The students were slowly learning to trust the adults around them, and to regulate their emotions. Cooperative activities were increasing with success. There was less refusal to engage in simple academic tasks. These were not small changes to them; they were transformative.

It became clear that measuring them only against the expectations for their chronological age or curriculum level was not just unhelpful — it was misleading. These children were making huge strides, but because the starting point was different for each of them, their progress only became visible when I compared them to their own earlier selves. That is when I began to understand the power of ipsative assessment.

The Limitations of Standardised Benchmarks

As discussed earlier in Chapter 3, progress is too often defined by standardised benchmarks, whether national standards, curriculum levels, or externally imposed "expected" progress rates. These measures are designed to create a common frame of reference, allowing governments and agencies to compare data across schools, regions, and even countries. While this can serve a purpose for policy monitoring and broad system accountability, it is an inherently blunt instrument when applied to individual learners.

The central limitation lies in the assumption that all children can and should be measured against the same yardstick, at the same points in time. This ignores the complex and uneven nature of human development. A child who begins school with significant developmental delays, disrupted early education, or the impacts of trauma and neurodiversity may make extraordinary progress within a year, yet still fall short of the fixed "expected" benchmark. In such cases, the official record may show them as "behind," even though their personal growth has been remarkable. Over time, this can send a harmful and repeated message: *you are not meeting the mark*, which risks becoming internalised into a child's sense of self-worth (Hattie, 2009; OECD, 2019).

Conversely, for students who consistently meet or exceed these benchmarks, the narrative of success can be equally limiting. Learning becomes framed as a competitive race to stay ahead, encouraging surface-level performance rather than depth of understanding or curiosity-driven exploration (Kohn, 1999). When "exceeding expectations" is the only celebrated outcome, the incentive to take risks, engage in creative thinking, or persevere through challenging learning diminishes.

Benchmarks, by their very design, strip away the nuance of personal growth. They are ill-equipped to capture progress that does not fit neatly into linear trajectories, such as the development of problem-solving strategies, resilience, or collaboration skills - qualities that the OECD (2018) and World Economic Forum (2020) identify as critical for thriving in the 21st century. The result is a narrowing of what counts as learning, privileging easily measurable outcomes over those that are harder to quantify but equally vital.

The irony is that the same tools intended to "raise standards" can sometimes obscure the very progress they aim to promote. This is where ipsative assessment, measuring a learner's growth against their own prior performance, becomes a powerful counterbalance. By shifting the focus from *where you are compared to everyone else* to *how far you have come*, it offers a more authentic, motivating, and human-centred way to understand progress.

What is Ipsative Assessment?

Ipsative assessment shifts the focus from external comparison to self-referenced progress. Rather than asking, *"How do you compare to others?"*, the central question becomes, *"How far have you come?"* This subtle but profound change reframes the purpose of assessment from ranking and sorting learners to understanding and celebrating individual growth over time (Hughes, 2011; Brown, 2013).

The concept of "personal best" lies at the heart of this approach. In fields such as athletics, music performance, or skill-based trades, progress has traditionally been tracked against the individual's own previous efforts rather than against others. Athletes celebrate shaving half a second off a sprint time; musicians value being able to play a previously impossible passage. These are not judged in comparison to the world's fastest runner or most accomplished pianist, but in terms of *personal improvement*. Each small gain represents momentum, builds confidence, and reinforces persistence. Education can learn from this tradition.

Psychological research supports the power of personal best goals. Martin and Elliot (2015) argue that setting goals relative to one's own past performance strengthens intrinsic motivation, fosters resilience, and enhances engagement, particularly in contexts where learners may otherwise feel discouraged by comparison with external benchmarks. When learners can see and celebrate incremental progress, even if they are not yet "at standard," they are more likely to persist, develop a growth mindset, and build academic buoyancy.

In classrooms, this means that ipsative assessment does more than complement formative assessment (Black & Wiliam, 1998). It sharpens its lens, focusing not just on the gap between current performance and an external criterion, but on the learner's own trajectory. This makes it particularly powerful for those students whose starting points are far below benchmark expectations. Instead of internalising deficit labels, they can see and take pride in measurable progress that is *theirs*. Equally, students who are already high-achieving can use ipsative approaches to stretch themselves beyond "easy wins" toward deeper mastery, avoiding complacency (Deci & Ryan, 2000).

In practice, ipsative assessment might take the form of growth trackers, portfolios, learning journals, or regular student-teacher conferences where past and present work is compared. It invites a different kind of dialogue: *"Look at where you were six weeks ago, and look at where you are now. What changed? What worked? What's next?"* Such conversations centre the learner as an active participant in their own development, making progress visible and meaningful.

Ultimately, ipsative assessment restores the human dimension to evaluation. It reminds us that every learner's journey is unique, and that progress is best understood not as a race against others but as an ongoing process of personal growth.

The benefits extend beyond motivation. Research indicates that self-referenced assessment can support the development of metacognitive skills, as learners become more aware of their strategies and growth patterns (Andrade & Brookhart, 2016). This in turn aligns closely with the OECD's (2018) call for assessment practices that not only measure outcomes but also equip learners with the capacity to reflect on and manage their own learning.

By placing the learner's past self as the point of reference, ipsative assessment resists the deficit narratives that fixed benchmarks can create. It enables teachers to frame progress as a personal journey, where each step forward is evidence of learning worth recognising.

The Benefits of Ipsative Assessment in Practice

When we measure progress against a learner's own starting point, several important benefits emerge:

- **PERSONALISED LEARNING JOURNEYS**

    Ipsative assessment recognises that no two learners begin from the same place.

    It allows teachers to design next steps that are genuinely responsive rather than formulaic.

- **REINFORCING STUDENT AGENCY**

    When students see tangible evidence of their own growth, they begin to set and own their learning goals. The motivation shifts from performing for external approval to striving for personal improvement.

- **BUILDING RESILIENCE AND SELF-BELIEF**

    Success becomes possible for everyone. The small but meaningful wins accumulate into a belief that effort makes a difference, countering the learned helplessness that fixed benchmark systems can create.

▶ **STRENGTHENING RELATIONSHIPS**

Conversations about growth become collaborative rather than judgemental. Teachers and students work together to recognise progress, celebrate it, and set new challenges.

Implementing Ipsative Assessment in a High-Accountability Context

One of the biggest challenges is integrating ipsative assessment in environments where external accountability systems dominate. High-stakes testing and standardised benchmarks create powerful incentives for schools to prioritise what is measurable, often at the expense of what is meaningful (Lingard, Martino, & Rezai-Rashti, 2017). In such climates, ipsative assessment can be perceived as secondary, because it does not yield the kind of comparative data policymakers demand. Yet, this perception underestimates its potential: ipsative assessment does not replace external measures, it complements them by telling a richer story about growth and learning.

In practice, the real work lies in balancing the tension between system demands and professional integrity. Teachers must often navigate dual accountabilities: to the benchmarks set by national systems, and to the young people in their classrooms.

Ipsative assessment helps preserve the latter without undermining the former. By documenting individual growth alongside mandated outcomes, teachers can provide evidence of progress that is both system-recognisable and deeply human.

This balancing act is not easy. It requires school leaders to create protective space for teachers to integrate alternative forms of assessment without fear of sanction. It also requires a reframing of accountability itself: from being solely about comparative performance, to being about whether every learner is moving forward from their starting point (Day & Smethem, 2009). In this sense, ipsative assessment can function as a subtle but powerful act of professional agency. It allows teachers to "play the game" of compliance while still affirming that their ultimate accountability is to their students' growth.

When viewed this way, ipsative assessment becomes more than just a method. It is a statement of values. It resists the flattening of students into scores and instead insists that progress, however small, matters. In high-accountability contexts, this stance is not an indulgence. It is essential to preserving the moral core of education.

Addressing Common Concerns and Misconceptions

"It's too subjective."

A common misconception about ipsative assessment is that it is simply a matter of teacher opinion. While teacher judgement is certainly involved, this does not mean the process is unstructured or arbitrary. Ipsative assessment can (and should) be anchored in transparent criteria, with progress documented over time using tools such as rubrics, annotated exemplars, learning logs, and photographic or video evidence.

Regular moderation between teachers further strengthens consistency, helping to align judgements and reduce variability. In many ways, ipsative assessment is no more subjective than marking a piece of creative writing or assessing oral language skills, both of which rely on professional judgement guided by clear indicators. The difference is that ipsative assessment uses that judgement to track growth, not just to determine whether a standard has been met.

"It won't work for reporting."

Another concern is that ipsative progress cannot be meaningfully reported to parents, whānau, or school leaders. In reality, many parents find this form of reporting far more valuable because it tells the story of their child's learning journey. Instead of a blunt indicator that says "at", "above" or "below" standard, they receive information about where their child started, the progress they have made, and what their next steps will be.

This narrative is especially powerful when combined with other reporting requirements, such as curriculum levels, NCEA progressions, or other mandated measures. Rather than replacing system-level data, ipsative assessment enriches it, giving families and leaders a fuller, more human picture of student achievement.

"It's only for struggling learners."

It's easy to assume that ipsative assessment is mainly a motivational tool for students who are behind expected benchmarks. While it can indeed be transformative for these learners, it is equally powerful for high-achieving students. When the only measure of success is meeting or exceeding an external standard, capable students may quickly reach a plateau, coasting without real challenge.

By asking high-achievers to set personal best goals, whether in the depth of analysis in an essay, the complexity of a science investigation, or the creativity of a performance.

Ipsative assessment pushes them beyond "easy wins" into genuinely stretching themselves. This prevents complacency and keeps learning engaging, even for those already working well above expectations.

A Call to Reimagine Success

At its heart, ipsative assessment challenges us to rethink what it means for a student to succeed. If the goal of education is to help every learner move forward from where they are now, then comparing them solely against others is not only insufficient, it risks obscuring the progress that matters most.

For teachers, this approach reaffirms professional autonomy. It validates their deep knowledge of their students and recognises that some forms of growth cannot be captured in a single test score. For students, it reframes education as a personal journey rather than a constant competition, fostering self-awareness, resilience, and a lifelong learning mindset.

The choice is not a binary one between system measures and ipsative assessment. It is about refusing to allow a single, narrow definition of progress to dominate the narrative. By adopting approaches that value personal growth, we send a powerful message to students: *who you are becoming matters more than how you compare.*

CHAPTER FIVE REFERENCES:

Andrade, H. L., & Brookhart, S. M. (2016). *The role of classroom assessment in supporting self-regulated learning.* In D. L. De Jong, L. Allal, & D. L. Butler (Eds.), *Handbook of self-regulation of learning and performance* (pp. 339–351). Routledge.

Ball, S. J., Maguire, M., & Braun, A. (2012). *How schools do policy: Policy enactments in secondary schools.* Routledge.

Black, P., & Wiliam, D. (1998). Assessment and classroom learning. *Assessment in Education: Principles, Policy & Practice, 5*(1), 7–74. https://doi.org/10.1080/0969595980050102

Brown, G. T. L. (2013). The validity of examination-based assessment for accountability: The case of New Zealand. *Assessment in Education: Principles, Policy & Practice, 20*(1), 89–105. https://doi.org/10.1080/0969594X.2012.733042

Day, C., & Smethem, L. (2009). The effects of reform: Have teachers really lost their sense of professionalism? *Journal of Educational Change, 10*(2–3), 141–157. https://doi.org/10.1007/s10833-009-9110-5

Deci, E. L., & Ryan, R. M. (2000). The "what" and "why" of goal pursuits: Human needs and the self-determination of behavior. *Psychological Inquiry, 11*(4), 227–268. https://doi.org/10.1207/S15327965PLI1104_01

Hattie, J. (2009). *Visible learning: A synthesis of over 800 meta-analyses relating to achievement.* Routledge.

Hughes, G. (2011). Towards a personal best: A case for introducing Ipsative assessment: in higher education. *Studies in Higher Education, 36*(3), 353-367.

Kohn, A. (1999). *The schools our children deserve: Moving beyond traditional classrooms and "tougher standards".* Houghton Mifflin.

Lingard, B., Martino, W., & Rezai-Rashti, G. (2017). Testing regimes, accountabilities and education policy: Commensurate global and national developments. *Journal of Education Policy, 32*(5), 611–621. https://doi.org/10.1080/02680939.2017.1311033

Martin, A. J., & Elliot, A. J. (2015). The role of personal best (PB) goal setting in students' academic achievement gains. *Learning and Individual Differences, 45.*

OECD. (2018). *The future of education and skills: Education 2030.* OECD Publishing. From https://www.oecd.org/content/dam/oecd/en/publications/reports/2018/06/the- future-of-education-and-skills_5424dd26/54ac7020-en.pdf

OECD. (2019). *OECD skills outlook 2019: Thriving in a digital world.* OECD Publishing. From https://www.oecd.org/content/dam/oecd/en/publications/reports/2019/05/oecd- skills-strategy-2019_g1g9ff20/9789264313835-en.pdf

World Economic Forum. (2020). *Schools of the future: Defining new models of education for the fourth industrial revolution.* World Economic Forum. https://www.weforum.org/reports/schools-of-the-future

Chapter Six
Reclaiming Your Agency

"If I don't do what the policy says, I'll get in trouble."

That's what a teacher whispered to me during a workshop last year. She had thirty sets of eyes watching her every move, but she was looking at me like someone desperate for permission. Permission to do what she knew was right for her students. Permission to use her professional judgement.

It's a moment I've seen countless times. Policy dictates one thing, experience tells us another, and somewhere between the two a teacher's agency quietly erodes. But here's the truth: you can reclaim it — not by breaking rules, but by understanding your power, identifying your sphere of influence, and taking intentional steps to act within it.

Knowing Your Sphere of Influence

Stephen Covey (1989) has written about the *circle of concern* and the *circle of influence*. In teaching, your circle of concern is vast: government policies, budget cuts, public perception, curriculum mandates, school politics, the wellbeing of every child in your care. But your circle of influence - the space where you can *actually* act - is closer and more powerful than you might think.

Practical Action:

- List three things you *can* control right now (e.g., the way you plan lessons, how you greet students at the door, the resources you choose).
- Commit to focusing your energy here first, before letting external pressures drain your capacity.

Practising Micro-Resistance

Agency isn't always about large acts of defiance. More often, it lives in the quiet, intentional choices teachers make every day to protect the integrity of their practice. These seemingly small decisions - how you adapt a mandated activity, the moments you create for curiosity, the gentle deflection of an unnecessary demand - are acts of *micro-resistance*.

Educational research describes micro-resistance as the everyday, localised strategies that educators use to uphold their professional values and pedagogical priorities under pressure. Albin-Clark et al., (2023) found that early childhood educators frequently engaged in such "atomised" acts of micro-resistance, subtly adjusting their practice in ways that preserved their commitment to child-centred learning despite external expectations. These were rarely grand gestures; instead, they were small, purposeful interventions that kept their pedagogy intact. Even in the face of rigid assessment requirements, teachers found ways to embed moments of joy, exploration, and agency into the learning environment, ensuring that the assessment did not completely override their pedagogical vision.

These studies remind us that micro-resistance is not about avoiding accountability. It's about preserving the conditions for authentic learning to flourish. In times when professional autonomy feels under threat, these small acts are vital threads in the fabric of teacher agency. They are how we quietly, but powerfully, keep good pedagogy alive in our classrooms (Albin-Clark & Archer, 2023).

Examples of Micro-Resistance:

- Embedding culturally sustaining practices even if they're not in the official unit plan.
- Keeping space in your timetable for student-led projects.
- Using mandated assessment tools in a way that also gives you formative, meaningful insights.

These actions don't ignore compliance requirements. They work *around* them to safeguard what you know matters most.

Reclaiming Classroom Decision-Making

You are the expert in your room. The best policy in the world can't predict the needs of the child sitting in front of you today. No framework, curriculum, or assessment schedule can see the expression on their face, the tension in their shoulders, or the unspoken questions in their eyes. That's your role, and it's where your professional expertise matters most.

Classroom decision-making is the daily exercise of teacher agency: the moment-to-moment judgments that shape learning experiences. Teacher agency is enacted *in situ*, dependent on the interplay between individual capacity, available resources, and the immediate context. This means your decisions are not just about applying policy, they are about interpreting it through the lens of your professional knowledge, your relationships with students, and your understanding of what will work *here, today* (Priestley, Biesta, and Robinson, 2015).

Why Decision-Making Matters

When decision-making is eroded, whether through scripted lessons, excessive testing, or rigid pacing guides, teaching risks becoming an act of compliance rather than a craft of responsiveness. Research warns that when teachers are denied autonomy, not only does their job satisfaction decrease, but so too does the quality of learning for students (Pearson & Moomaw, 2005). Conversely, when teachers retain decision-making authority, they can adapt content, adjust timing, and shift methods to meet the dynamic needs of their learners.

Everyday Acts of Professional Judgement

Reclaiming classroom decision-making doesn't necessarily mean rejecting all external direction. It means holding onto the *how*. The ways you bring policy to life in your context. For example:

- Adjusting sequence and pace so that a concept is deeply understood before moving on.
- Embedding culturally responsive practices that reflect the identities and
- languages of your learners, even if not explicitly mentioned in the curriculum.
- Balancing explicit instruction with exploratory learning, ensuring students not only know but also think, question, and create.

These acts of professional judgement are often subtle, yet they are foundational to quality teaching. As Sachs (2001) argues, the capacity to shape the curriculum in context is a defining feature of a democratic, professional teaching force.

Linking to Micro-Resistance

In the current policy climate, reclaiming decision-making can be a form of micro-resistance. When a mandated programme tells you exactly what to say, your decision to pause for a rich student-led discussion is an act of protection, for both the learner's agency and your own professional integrity. When the timetable is crowded, and you carve out space for a hands-on investigation or a story that sparks empathy, you are resisting the drift toward a narrowed, test-driven experience.

Your Challenge

Reclaiming classroom decision-making starts with noticing the moments where you *do* have choice, however small. From there, it's about exercising those choices deliberately and reflecting on their impact. This isn't about ignoring accountability. It's about ensuring accountability includes the quality of thought, care, and responsiveness you bring to your practice.

The more teachers reclaim their decision-making, the more we collectively shift the narrative away from standardisation toward professional trust. One teacher making thoughtful, context-driven choices can create ripples. An entire profession doing so can change the tide.

Strategies:

- Co-design learning with students: Invite them to shape questions, formats, and outcomes within the curriculum parameters.
- Use "both/and" thinking: Deliver required content *and* weave in curiosity, play, and creativity.
- Keep professional notes: Document your decisions, your rationale, and evidence of student progress. This protects you if questioned and builds a portfolio of practice you can be proud of.

Leveraging Collaboration

Isolation fuels compliance. Collaboration fuels confidence. When you work in isolation, it's easier to doubt your judgement, to wonder if your hesitation over a mandated approach is just you "being difficult." But when you talk with colleagues, you quickly realise that many share your frustrations, your questions, and, crucially, your hopes.

Collaboration is more than sharing resources or taking turns at playground duty. Done well, it is a process of collective sense-making. Testing ideas, exploring alternatives, and supporting each other to take professional risks. Hargreaves and O'Connor (2018) describe *collaborative professionalism* as a process where educators "work together with deep respect, collective responsibility, and mutual accountability to achieve what is best for students." This is collaboration with purpose, not just collegiality for its own sake.

Why Collaboration Counters Compliance

Compliance thrives when decision-making is private and invisible. When no one sees you adapt a lesson, change an assessment, or pause for student-led inquiry, it's easier for external control to remain unchallenged. Collaboration brings those decisions into the open. It gives permission to discuss *why* something doesn't work and to co-create alternatives that do.

Research suggests that collaborative cultures not only strengthen teacher agency, but also improve student outcomes (Vangrieken et al., 2015). In schools where teachers engage in professional dialogue, particularly across year levels and subject areas, there is greater alignment between teaching practices and the needs of learners, without sacrificing creativity or context.

Building a Culture of Professional Dialogue

Leveraging collaboration for confidence and agency means creating spaces where professional dialogue is not just tolerated but actively encouraged. That might look like:

- Structured peer observation cycles that focus on shared learning rather than evaluation.

- Cross-curricular teams exploring how a policy directive plays out differently in different contexts.
- Regular 'what's working' sessions where teachers share small acts of adaptation or innovation.
- Critical friend partnerships - a trusted colleague you can test ideas with before making changes in your classroom.

The key is psychological safety (Edmondson, 2019). Teachers need to know they can speak honestly without fear of judgement or reprisal. Without that trust, collaboration risks becoming performative surface-level sharing without genuine growth.

Collaboration as Collective Micro-Resistance

When collaboration is underpinned by trust and shared purpose, it can also become a form of collective micro-resistance. A group of teachers agreeing to maintain daily opportunities for child-led inquiry despite timetable pressures is not just preserving a pedagogy, it's protecting a research-backed practice that nurtures agency and curiosity. A team deciding to interpret a rigid policy in ways that retain space for creativity is using the power of the group to resist the erosion of professional judgement.

This doesn't mean forming an "us versus them" mindset. It means understanding that strong professional communities create the conditions for thoughtful, values-driven action, even when navigating externally imposed constraints.

Ways to Collaborate for Agency:

- Form a "pedagogy circle" with trusted colleagues to explore creative, research- informed ways of teaching mandated content while staying true to your values.

- Share successful lesson designs across departments or year levels to multiply the impact of innovative practice.

- Support one another in trialling small shifts - observe, offer constructive feedback, and celebrate successes together to build confidence and momentum.

- Document and reflect on collaborative wins so they can be shared with leadership or used to inform future policy discussions.

- Rotate leadership roles in collaborative groups to ensure everyone has the opportunity to shape the agenda and bring forward their expertise.

Reframing the Narrative

The dominant story told about teachers is too often one of underperformance, crisis, or blame. This deficit framing not only demoralises educators but also shapes public perception and policy in ways that erode trust and autonomy. Reframing the narrative doesn't mean ignoring challenges, it means actively choosing to highlight the strengths, successes, and positive impacts of teaching.

By deliberately telling different stories, you can help shift the conversation from one of failure to one of possibility. These stories matter: they influence how students see themselves, how families engage with schools, and how policymakers design education systems.

Reframing in action might look like this:

- Share successes with whānau, not just problems. Make sure parents and caregivers hear about moments of joy, achievement, and growth, not only behavioural issues or academic concerns. This helps them see the richness of their child's learning journey.

- Tell your own teaching story at staff meetings. Rather than only reporting data or compliance updates, use these opportunities to highlight what worked, why it worked, and how it made a difference for your students.

- Challenge deficit language when you hear it. If safe to do so, gently reframe comments like "these kids can't…" into strengths-based statements that recognise potential, resilience, and progress.
- Curate evidence of impact. Keep a record of positive feedback, student work, or classroom moments that demonstrate learning and growth. These artefacts can be powerful advocacy tools when engaging with leadership or policymakers.
- Model the narrative you want others to adopt. Use social media, newsletters, and community events to tell a balanced, hopeful story about education in your context.

When teachers collectively reframe the narrative, they reclaim the power to define what good teaching looks like and remind the world that education is about more than meeting benchmarks; it's about enabling human flourishing.

Teaching on Your Terms

Reclaiming your agency isn't about fighting every policy or taking on every battle. It's about *choosing*, carefully, strategically, where you will stand your ground, and then holding that ground with integrity.

Tomorrow morning, when you walk into your classroom, remember:

- You *are* the expert in the room.
- You have choices, even within constraints.
- Every small act of professional courage creates ripples far beyond your classroom walls.

Agency isn't given to you. It's something you take back, step by step, conversation by conversation, lesson by lesson. And the future of education depends on teachers like you doing just that.

Chapter Six References

Albin-Clark, J., & Archer, N. (2023). *Resisting intensified accountability: Is now the time for inspection reform?* Early Education. Retrieved August 25, 2025, from https://early-education.org.uk/resisting-intensified-accountability

Covey, S. R. (1989). *The 7 habits of highly effective people.* Free Press.

Edmondson, A. C. (2019). *The fearless organization: Creating psychological safety in the workplace for learning, innovation, and growth.* Wiley.

Hargreaves, A., & O'Connor, M. T. (2018). *Collaborative professionalism: When teaching together means learning for all.* Corwin.

Pearson, L. C., & Moomaw, W. (2005). The relationship between teacher autonomy and stress, work satisfaction, empowerment, and professionalism. *Educational Research Quarterly, 29*(1), 38–54.

Priestley, M., Biesta, G. J. J., & Robinson, S. (2015). *Teacher agency: An ecological approach.* Bloomsbury.

Sachs, J. (2001). Teacher professional identity: Competing discourses, competing outcomes. *Journal of Education Policy, 16*(2), 149–161. https://doi.org/10.1080/02680930116819

Vangrieken, K., Dochy, F., Raes, E., & Kyndt, E. (2015). Teacher collaboration: A systematic review. *Educational Research Review, 15*, 17–40. https://doi.org/10.1016/j.edurev.2015.04.002

Chapter Seven

Teaching as a Human Science

Sam's Story: Seeing the Human First

Sam was a Year 8 boy who sat at the back of the classroom with a thunder cloud over his face most days. He didn't particularly like reading, wasn't too fussed on maths, and definitely didn't see the point to the unit of study we were focused on: Aboriginal Australia. Early in the school year, he announced that he had no interest in anything apart from becoming a truck driver, just like his dad and his grandad before him. He planned to be down at the truck yard every weekend and after school, cleaning trucks and learning the ropes. In his eyes, there was no point learning anything unrelated to trucks.

I could have stuck to the script, followed the programme, and expected compliance despite his lack of motivation or engagement. But he needed a human connection. Someone who saw him, respected what mattered to him, and nurtured that spark.

Instead of forcing him through the prescribed unit, I worked with Sam to create a learning plan anchored in his passion. He began studying the road code, learning about heavy vehicle licensing, and exploring everything he could about trucks. His maths became relevant, grounded in mileage, tonnage, fuel consumption, and other calculations related to the logistics industry. His goal was to pass a pretend truck driver's licence with me by the end of the year.

The change was remarkable. His engagement soared, his motivation became visible, and his sense of self-worth grew. In that classroom, Sam became a valued person because school made sense to him.

Sam's story isn't about lowering expectations. It's about humanising education. Recognising that teaching is as much about knowing the learner as it is about knowing (and delivering) the curriculum, and that relevance can be the bridge to both engagement and achievement.

What It Means to Teach as a Human Science

Teaching is too often framed in the language of efficiency, performance, and measurement. Policies and reforms cast it as if it were an industrial process, with inputs (curriculum content), controls (compliance systems), and outputs (test scores). This framing is seductive because it offers neatness and measurability, but it misses the heart of the matter. Teaching is not simply a technical act; it is a profoundly human one.

The German philosopher Wilhelm Dilthey distinguished between the *Naturwissenschaften* (natural sciences) and the *Geisteswissenschaften* (human sciences). Natural sciences such as physics or chemistry seek universal laws through controlled observation. Human sciences, by contrast, concern themselves with meaning, culture, and lived experience (Dilthey, 1910/2002). Education sits firmly within this second tradition. It is concerned not just with what students know, but with who they are becoming - their identities, relationships, aspirations, and sense of belonging.

If teaching is a human science, then the classroom is not a factory floor but a living community. Pedagogical theorists like Max van Manen (2015) have long argued that teaching is fundamentally moral and relational, because it involves responsibility for the growth and flourishing of another human being. This means the work of teaching can never be reduced to scripts or standardised delivery models. Instead, it demands attentiveness, empathy, and professional judgement in the moment as teachers interpret the needs of the learner in front of them.

Hannah Arendt (1961) described education as the place where adults introduce children to the world - a responsibility that is at once protective and generative. It asks teachers to hold on to what is of value in our shared world while preparing young people to renew and reshape it in ways appropriate to their time. Jerome Bruner (1996) added another important insight: that human beings make sense of the world through story and narrative. Learning, then, is not only about acquiring skills or knowledge but about weaving personal and cultural stories into shared understanding. These philosophical anchors remind us that the human science of teaching requires us to attend to meaning, not merely to metrics.

Welby Ings (2017) extends this conversation in the Aotearoa context, describing effective teachers as those who teach from the inside out. By this he means that authentic pedagogy arises from who the teacher is, not just what they deliver. Ings argues that transformative teaching happens in the grey spaces between compliance and creativity, where professional judgement and humanity guide decisions more than policy. He cautions against the rise of "educational monocultures" that prize uniformity over responsiveness, noting that real learning often emerges when teachers notice the unexpected and adapt with courage.

Contemporary research echoes these ideas. Vygotsky (1978) described learning as an inherently social process mediated through interaction, scaffolding, and dialogue. Freire (1970) urged educators to resist the "banking model" of education, instead cultivating a dialogic practice that honours learners' lived realities. Nel Noddings (2013) added an ethical dimension with her ethic of care, highlighting that authentic, reciprocal relationships form the foundation of learning. Neuroscience further supports this view: Perry and Szalavitz (2010) show that trust, safety, and emotional connection activate the very neural systems that make deep learning possible.

In Aotearoa, the research of Bishop and Berryman (2006) underscores the same principle in a local context. When teachers design learning that affirms cultural identity and builds relational trust, engagement and achievement rise, particularly for Māori learners. This illustrates how culture and identity are not optional extras but central to the conditions in which learning flourishes.

To see teaching as a human science is to honour the unpredictability and complexity of learning. It is to acknowledge that while structure and evidence-based practices are important, they must always serve the learner rather than the other way around. This stance does not reject accountability. Instead, it reframes accountability in human terms: are we helping learners grow, belong, and flourish?

When we adopt this perspective, we create classrooms where meaning-making is alive, where identity is affirmed, and where curiosity is not crowded out by compliance. This is not just an intellectual argument. It is a moral imperative for teachers who know that their daily work is about far more than covering content. It is about shaping the conditions in which children can grow as whole human beings.

Practical Ways to Teach as a Human Science

The human science of teaching is lived out in the daily choices we make with our students. It is about noticing the individuals in front of us and shaping learning in ways that recognise their context, strengths, and aspirations. This doesn't require abandoning curriculum goals; it requires bringing them to life in ways that matter to the learner.

1. SEE THE PERSON FIRST

Before planning interventions or designing lessons, ask yourself: *Who is this learner beyond the data?* What lights them up? What do they talk about when they feel safe? What do they see as important in their life now and in the future?

When you take the time to notice and honour these aspects, the relationship shifts. Students are far more likely to engage, even in subjects they have previously resisted, when they feel recognised as more than their achievement levels. Seeing the person first means recognising their passions, values, cultural identity, and lived experiences as central to how they learn.

This approach doesn't mean abandoning curriculum expectations, but it does mean weaving them through the lens of what matters to the student. When learners feel that school acknowledges their reality, they are more open to stepping into ours. It is a reciprocal exchange, one built on trust, dignity, and mutual respect.

2. Connect Curriculum to Identity

When students see themselves reflected in their learning, they are more likely to see it as relevant to their lives. This isn't just about adding the occasional cultural reference or a themed activity. It's about designing learning in a way that affirms and sustains the diverse identities in the room, weaving together the curriculum with the lived realities of your learners.

Culturally sustaining pedagogy (Paris & Alim, 2017) takes this further by deliberately nurturing and extending the cultural and linguistic practices students bring with them. It recognises that identity is dynamic, shaped by heritage, community, relationships, and personal passions. For some learners, like Sam, their passion might be occupational or practical; for others, it might be deeply tied to cultural heritage or whānau traditions.

Curriculum, then, becomes less of a rigid sequence to "get through" and more of a framework to be inhabited with meaning. This approach invites you to ask:

- *Whose stories are we telling here?*
- *Whose perspectives are missing?*
- *How can this content be anchored in local context, community history, or the aspirations of our learners?*

When we fail to make these connections, students can experience a subtle erosion of self, a feeling that their culture, language, or way of knowing is peripheral to "real learning." Over time, this can undermine motivation and belonging. When we succeed, we affirm the whole person.

Consider how this plays out in practical terms:

- A mathematics unit on measurement becomes an exploration of traditional navigation techniques used by Pacific voyagers.
- A science topic on ecology incorporates local Māori knowledge of native species and seasonal patterns.
- A literacy unit draws on contemporary and historical voices from the students' own communities, encouraging them to author work that reflects their lived experience.

These connections not only improve engagement but also deepen understanding. When learners are invited to engage through their cultural frames of reference, they bring more of themselves to the task - their humour, values, worldviews, and creativity.

This is not "extra" work to be tacked on after the curriculum is planned. It *is* the work of teaching. Seeing identity as central to curriculum design helps us avoid tokenism and instead create spaces where learning affirms who students are, and who they are becoming.

3. Value Process Over Product

A human science approach to teaching sees learning not as a straight line toward a fixed end point, but as an unfolding journey. This journey is often messy, full of trial, error, backtracking, and unexpected breakthroughs. It is in this iterative process, the doing, un-doing, and re-doing, that deep learning often occurs.

When the focus is solely on the finished product, students can become risk-averse, reluctant to experiment for fear of producing something "wrong." By shifting emphasis toward the process, we invite learners to engage more fully with the experience, to take intellectual and creative risks, and to see mistakes as integral stepping stones rather than evidence of inadequacy.

Research into growth mindset (Dweck, 2006) supports this approach, showing that when students believe their abilities can develop through effort, strategy, and feedback, they are more resilient in the face of challenge. Valuing process also aligns with experiential learning theory (Kolb, 1984), which underscores the importance of reflection and adaptation as part of the learning cycle.

A process-focused classroom might:

- Encourage students to share drafts, prototypes, or "half-formed" ideas with peers.
- Use feedback loops where revisions are expected and celebrated.
- Allocate time for reflection on *how* a learner approached a task, not just *what* they produced.
- Incorporate self-assessment, helping students articulate the strategies and decisions behind their work.

This shift is particularly powerful when connected to identity and humanity. A student's process is shaped by their cultural background, prior experiences, and ways of knowing.

Recognising and valuing those diverse pathways to understanding affirms the learner's identity in the same way as connecting curriculum content to their life context.

It also reframes assessment. Instead of viewing the teacher as the sole evaluator of worth, the process invites co-agency. Students become active participants in deciding what success looks like for them. This doesn't mean abandoning standards, but it does mean broadening what counts as evidence of learning and acknowledging the richness of the journey.

In the end, valuing process over product is about seeing students not as empty vessels to be filled, but as capable agents in their own learning. It is a stance that prioritises curiosity, resilience, and reflection, qualities that serve them long after the specifics of any single lesson have faded.

4. MAKE SPACE FOR AUTONOMY

Autonomy is one of the most powerful drivers of human motivation. Self-determination theory (Deci & Ryan, 2000) identifies autonomy, the ability to have some control over one's actions, as a core psychological need alongside competence and relatedness. When learners feel that they have a voice in how they approach a task, their engagement and investment deepen.

In a human science approach, autonomy is not about handing over all control or abandoning structure. Rather, it is about recognising students as active partners in the learning process. Even small acts of choice, such as selecting from a range of texts, choosing the format for presenting an idea, or helping to co-design an assessment rubric, can signal to students that their perspectives matter. These choices affirm their agency and signal trust in their capacity to make decisions.

Autonomy also connects deeply to identity. When students influence the direction of their learning, they can bring aspects of their culture, passions, and lived experiences into the classroom. This fosters a sense of belonging, because learning no longer feels like something done *to* them, but rather something they are actively shaping. For learners whose voices have historically been marginalised, these moments of decision- making can be especially powerful acts of self-definition and reclamation.

Practically, making space for autonomy might look like:

- Providing open-ended inquiry prompts that students can adapt to their own interests.
- Offering multiple pathways for demonstrating understanding. For example, through writing, visual art, oral storytelling, or digital media.
- Allowing students to set personal goals within a larger project framework.
- Building in reflection time for students to articulate why they made certain choices and how those decisions influenced their learning.

Importantly, autonomy does not mean an absence of guidance. In a human science model, teachers act as wayfinders shaping the environment, providing scaffolds, and offering feedback, while ensuring that students retain meaningful influence over their own trajectory. Growth happens not by constraining learners or limiting their possibilities, but by equipping them with the confidence and skills to take flight in their own direction.

When students have autonomy, they not only learn the content at hand - they also develop the self-direction, adaptability, and problem-solving skills that will serve them in the unpredictable landscapes beyond school. Autonomy is, in this way, both a human right in learning and a lifelong competency.

5. USE RELATIONSHIPS AS THE DELIVERY SYSTEM

Educational theorists like Noddings (2013) have long argued that caring relationships are not an "add-on" to academic work; they are the foundation upon which learning rests. In her ethic of care, Noddings emphasises that genuine education is impossible without a relational connection between teacher and learner. It is through trust, respect, and emotional safety that the brain is freed to take the risks necessary for learning.

The neuroscience aligns with this view. The human brain is highly sensitive to perceived threat, whether physical or social. A classroom where a student feels judged, unsafe, or invisible will trigger protective behaviours rather than curiosity and engagement.

Conversely, when a student feels valued and understood, their stress response lowers, opening the cognitive space needed for focus, problem-solving, and creativity (Perry & Szalavitz, 2010).

Relationships in this sense are not simply about being "nice" or "friendly." They involve a deliberate practice of seeing and responding to students as whole people, not just as learners of a subject. This includes:

- Listening deeply and without interruption when students speak.
- Noticing shifts in mood or energy and adjusting expectations accordingly.
- Remembering and referencing details from their lives outside of school, signalling that they matter beyond their academic output.
- Communicating high expectations alongside high support, or a "warm demander" stance (Hammond, 2015).

A human science approach also recognises that relationships are dynamic and reciprocal. Teachers are not distant technicians delivering content; they are co-participants in the learning environment. Sharing appropriate aspects of one's own learning journey, struggles, and values helps humanise the teacher, allowing students to see the person behind the role. This authenticity fosters mutual respect, breaking down the "us" and "them" barrier that can alienate learners.

For some students, particularly those whose experiences with authority have been marked by mistrust or marginalisation, the teacher-student relationship may be the decisive factor in whether they engage with learning at all. This is why relationship- building is not an optional extra to be "fitted in" when time allows. It is the delivery system for everything else. The curriculum, assessment, and pedagogy all travel through the medium of relationship, and if that medium is fractured, the rest will struggle to take hold.

Transformation in education cannot be forced through pressure or coercion. True change emerges when teachers create conditions where learners feel safe, valued, and invited into growth. Relationships become that fertile ground - a space where students are seen, heard, and trusted enough to take risks and step into the unknown (Ings, 2017).

CHAPTER SEVEN REFERENCES

Arendt, H. (1961). *Between past and future: Eight exercises in political thought.* Viking Press.

Bishop, R., & Berryman, M. (2006). *Culture speaks: Cultural relationships and classroom learning.* Huia Publishers.

Bruner, J. (1996). *The culture of education.* Harvard University Press.

Deci, E. L., & Ryan, R. M. (2000). The "what" and "why" of goal pursuits: Human needs and the self-determination of behavior. *Psychological Inquiry, 11*(4), 227–268. https://doi.org/10.1207/S15327965PLI1104_01

Dilthey, W. (2002). *The formation of the historical world in the human sciences* (R. A. Makkreel & F. Rodi, Eds.). Princeton University Press. (Original work published 1910)

Dweck, C. S. (2006). *Mindset: The new psychology of success.* Random House. Freire, P. (1970). *Pedagogy of the oppressed.* Continuum.

Hammond, Z. (2015). *Culturally responsive teaching and the brain: Promoting authentic engagement and rigor among culturally and linguistically diverse students.* Corwin.

Ings, W. (2017). *Disobedient teaching: Surviving and thriving in a leadership role.* Otago University Press.

Kolb, D. A. (1984). *Experiential learning: Experience as the source of learning and development.* Prentice-Hall.

Noddings, N. (2013). *Caring: A relational approach to ethics and moral education* (2nd ed.). University of California Press.

Paris, D., & Alim, H. S. (2017). *Culturally sustaining pedagogies: Teaching and learning for justice in a changing world.* Teachers College Press.

Perry, B. D., & Szalavitz, M. (2010). *Born for love: Why empathy is essential—and endangered.* HarperCollins.

van Manen, M. (2015). *Pedagogical tact: Knowing what to do when you don't know what to do.* Routledge.

Vygotsky, L. S. (1978). *Mind in society: The development of higher psychological processes.* Harvard University Press.

Chapter Eight
An Invitation To Teachers

Trust, Not Permission

The invitation to reclaim the human science of teaching is not an invitation to recklessness. It is an invitation to conscious, ethical, and informed flexibility. It asks you to trust yourself, your values, and the knowledge of your learners more than you trust the shifting tides of policy. It is a call to return to the heart of the profession: teaching as a deeply human act.

This invitation is not about ignoring system requirements or disregarding accountability. Rather, it is about how you interpret them. The question is not *"Will you follow the rules?"* but *"How will you keep the learner at the centre while doing so?"* Every teacher already makes countless interpretive decisions in their day. This chapter is about making those decisions intentionally, courageously, and collectively.

The Myth of Permission

Too often, teachers are made to feel that they must wait for permission: permission from the Ministry, from the Board, from a principal, from policy. The myth of permission is powerful because it makes educators passive. It suggests that agency is something that will be "given" one day when conditions improve.

But in reality, agency is already here. Teachers act on it every day when they make choices about language, resources, groupings, or the framing of a lesson. There are schools across Aotearoa that are already living this invitation. They are not waiting for a policy shift. They are doing what others claim is impossible. They are showing that it is possible to meet curriculum goals while also nurturing joy, curiosity, and belonging.

These schools are not exceptions because they are privileged or uniquely resourced. They are exceptional because they have chosen to prioritise humanity alongside accountability. Their teachers collaborate to protect space for creativity, to adapt mandated requirements into meaningful experiences, and to advocate for children's holistic growth. Every one of these choices is a reminder that transformation does not begin with a new law or framework. It begins with teachers and leaders daring to interpret education through a human lens.

What This Looks Like in Practice

The invitation can be broken into practical commitments:

- **Know your learners deeply.** Understand their histories, strengths, fears and aspirations. Use this knowledge to shape relevant and respectful learning experiences.

- **Practise micro-resistance.** When a directive undermines good pedagogy, look for small, intentional acts that protect the learner experience without creating unnecessary conflict. This might mean adjusting timelines, rephrasing assessment criteria, or adding a layer of relevance to mandated content.

- **Collaborate for courage.** Isolation breeds compliance. Working with colleagues strengthens your resolve and generates creative solutions that meet both policy requirements and learner needs.

- **Anchor decisions in values.** When in doubt, ask: does this serve the learner's growth as a human being? Does this align with my professional ethics?

These are not radical actions. They are everyday professional decisions, grounded in integrity. Yet they accumulate into a culture where learners feel seen and teachers feel purposeful.

Epilogue to Sam's Story

Years after that transformative Year 8 experience, I unexpectedly crossed paths with Sam again. A family member happened to meet him, and when my name came up, his face lit up with recognition. He spoke with real energy about that year in school, recalling how his learning finally felt connected to his life and his dreams.

What stood out most was not the nostalgia, but the update. Sam was still driving trucks, but now he was in the middle of negotiating the purchase of his own trucking company. Nearly twenty years on from that first conversation about his future, he was making it happen.

This encounter was a powerful reminder that the connections we make with students can echo far beyond the school gates. When we teach the human first, we are not only impacting the moment, we may be shaping the trajectory of a life.

The Long View

In twenty years, your students will not remember the exact wording of a learning intention or the formatting of a worksheet. They will remember how they felt in your presence, the moments when you saw them, and the times you made learning feel possible and meaningful.

Sam's journey from disengaged Year 8 student to business owner in the trucking industry is not just a personal victory for him - it is a reminder that education's deepest work often unfolds long after the school years are over. Our influence as teachers is cumulative and sometimes invisible until much later.

Education is an act of faith (Ings, 2017). Teachers plant seeds of possibility without knowing which will flourish or when. This is why reclaiming the human science of teaching matters: because it ensures the seeds we plant are rooted in respect, relevance and relationship.

The Impossible Is Already Happening

Some may dismiss this vision as aspirational. They may say that in the face of national standards, benchmarks, and political pressures, human-centred teaching is unrealistic. But this is not true. All over Aotearoa, schools are already demonstrating that it is possible to both meet system requirements and protect joy, agency, and belonging.

- Schools are weaving local histories, reo, and cultural identities into curriculum delivery, making national frameworks come alive in ways that children recognise as their own.
- Schools are developing innovative assessment models that include portfolios and narrative reporting alongside mandated tests.
- Schools are carving out protected time for play, inquiry, or community projects, while still meeting achievement targets.

These are not hypothetical case studies. They are living examples of teachers and leaders choosing to interpret policy in ways that honour the learner first. They show us that the future of education does not need to wait for a government mandate. It is already unfolding in classrooms where teachers act with courage and conviction.

A Moral Centre for Teaching

Teaching well is rarely about sticking rigidly to black-and-white rules. The richest learning often happens in the in-between - the flexible, adaptive space where we draw on our experience, empathy, and creativity to respond to what is actually happening in the room.

This is why teaching is best understood as a human science. It is not about rejecting evidence-based practices, but about applying them with professional judgement. It is not about ignoring the curriculum, but about interpreting it so that it makes sense in this place, for these learners, at this time.

Good teaching emerges from the identity and integrity of the teacher. This is a reminder that professional integrity is not a luxury; it is a necessity. Without it, compliance becomes the driver and humanity slips away. With it, schools become spaces of belonging, creativity, and growth (Palmer, 1998)

A Call to Teachers

Sam's story is not unique. Every teacher has a "Sam" somewhere in their history. A learner who needed someone to see them, to make school make sense, to believe in them when they could not yet believe in themselves. These stories remind us that teaching is not a script to follow, but a relationship to nurture.

Policy can set parameters, but it cannot see the child in front of you today. Only you can do that. And that is where your real power lies.

Every day, you face a choice:

- To comply unquestioningly with what is handed down.
- Or to interpret it through the lens of humanity.
- To use your professional judgement.
- To teach in ways that make school meaningful for your learners.

This is not about ignoring requirements or acting recklessly. It is about teaching with integrity - choosing to be the kind of educator who balances mandates with meaning. Who knows that learning is richer when it grows from a learner's strengths, identity, and aspirations. Who refuses to let system compliance strip away connection and curiosity.

The Horizon Ahead

So here is the invitation:

- **Notice the human first.** Before the lesson plan, see the person in front of you.
- **Adapt without apology.** Tailor your teaching to serve the learner, even if it means bending the programme.
- **Protect curiosity.** Make room for wonder, questions, and joyful discovery, for them and for you.
- **Collaborate for courage.** Seek out colleagues who will support your agency and lend them your support in return.
- **Tell the good stories.** Share moments of success, growth, and humanity with your students, their families, and your peers.

The future of education will not be transformed by policy alone. It will be transformed by teachers who choose to see, value, and respond to the humanity in their classrooms every single day.

Your classroom is not just a place where knowledge is delivered. It is a place where lives are shaped, identities are affirmed, and futures are imagined. That is the power of teaching as a human act. That is your power.

Your Teacher Heart

The teacher heart has been the quiet anchor running beneath this book. Every story, every challenge, and every act of courage we have explored comes back to this central truth: teaching is not sustained by policy, programmes, or prescriptions. It is sustained by the deep well of care, curiosity, and commitment that sits at the core of every teacher.

The teacher heart is not sentimental. It is not about soft gestures or surface-level kindness. It is about the fierce determination to see and value young people, to hold hope for them when they cannot hold it for themselves, and to keep believing that education can be a place of transformation.

When we talk about reclaiming the human science of teaching, or practising micro- resistance, or reshaping assessment to reflect growth rather than ranking, these are not abstract pedagogical moves. They are acts of the teacher heart, in action. They are the daily choices that say: *I see you, I value you, and I will teach in ways that protect your dignity as a learner.*

The teacher heart is what enables us to walk into classrooms even when the system feels heavy. It is what gives us the courage to adapt, to resist, and to create moments of connection in the midst of constraint. It is what allows us to hold the long view, knowing that the seeds we plant today may not show their fruit for years to come.

This book began with the teacher heart and it ends here too, because that is where your true power lies. Long after policies shift and curricula change, the integrity of your heart as a teacher will remain the most powerful force in your classroom.

Chapter Eight References

Ings, W. (2017). *Disobedient teaching: Surviving and creating change in educational practice.* Otago University Press.

Palmer, P. J. (1998). *The courage to teach: Exploring the inner landscape of a teacher's life.* Jossey-Bass.

www.ingramcontent.com/pod-product-compliance
Lightning Source LLC
Chambersburg PA
CBHW062041290426
44109CB00026B/2700